ESCORTED AWAY!

HARRY JOSEPHSON

Copyright © 2023 Harry Josephson.

All rights reserved. No part of this book may be reproduced, stored, or transmitted by any means—whether auditory, graphic, mechanical, or electronic—without written permission of both publisher and author, except in the case of brief excerpts used in critical articles and reviews. Unauthorized reproduction of any part of this work is illegal and is punishable by law.

ISBN: 979-8-88640-908-6 (sc)
ISBN: 979-8-88640-909-3 (hc)
ISBN: 979-8-88640-910-9 (e)

Because of the dynamic nature of the Internet, any web addresses or links contained in this book may have changed since publication and may no longer be valid. The views expressed in this work are solely those of the author and do not necessarily reflect the views of the publisher, and the publisher hereby disclaims any responsibility for them.

One Galleria Blvd., Suite 1900, Metairie, LA 70001
1-888-421-2397

CONTENTS

Forward v

Chapter 1	The Pick-up 1
Chapter 2	The Child Who Almost Wasn't 4
Chapter 3	Sleepless Nights 9
Chapter 4	A Confused Little Boy 11
Chapter 5	Storm Warnings! 15
Chapter 6	"Weed" in the Closet and Into the Abyss 19
Chapter 7	The Car 20
Chapter 8	To "Insanity and Beyond" 22
Chapter 9	The Point of No Return 26
Chapter 10	Midwest Academy 28
Chapter 11	Coming Home September, 2006 46
Chapter 12	Heroin! 48
Chapter 13	Enabling and More Insanity 50
Chapter 14	Storm Clouds Over a New Marriage 52
Chapter 15	The Cash Stops (for now) 55
Chapter 16	April, 2010- Another DUI 57

Chapter 17	Nar-Anon and Al-Anon	59
Chapter 18	January 14, 2011 Free At Last?	67
Chapter 19	(2/18-3/14) Back to Jail!	70
Chapter 20	Packing and Moving "the Stuff"	73
Chapter 21	Back to Jail	75
Chapter 22	Quest Recovery-Wilson Hall	78
Chapter 23	My First Visit to Quest	80
Chapter 24	A Great Program	84
Chapter 25	Back Under Mom's Roof!	87
Chapter 26	Falling Apart and Going "Back Out"	90
Chapter 27	Glenbeigh	92
Chapter 28	Moving to Canton	95
Chapter 29	June 18, 2012 Back to Jail!	97
Chapter 30	Dad Checking Up	99
Chapter 31	32 Days in a Different Jail	102
Chapter 32	Wilson Hall II, August, 2012	105
Chapter 33	Establishing a New Life	106
Chapter 34	Ryan's "Lead"	110

What Have I Learned? 119

FORWARD

When I first started writing about my experiences with my son, Ryan and his difficulties, it was after he was "escorted" against his will, from my home near Columbus, Ohio, to a disciplinary boarding school in Keokuk, Iowa, back in 2005, when he had just turned 17 years old. This was where the title of the book came from. At that time, based upon what I was seeing in his progress in that program (which lasted nearly a year), I was hopeful that his experiences there would "straighten him out" so to speak, and that he would return a new person.

As of the date that I am writing this introduction, in September of 2011, just about 6 years have passed since the date described in Chapter 1. Many, many new experiences and "teaching moments", both for Ryan and me, have occurred since then. When he returned from the boarding school in 2006 on his 18th birthday, it was with the hope (on both our parts), that the problems were over, and that he would go on to live a productive life with college, a job, and maybe a family in his future. He seemed so changed by the experience that I was overcome with wishful thinking.

Not long after this date in 2006, at least based upon the story I was later told, is when he experimented with heroin for the first time, soon becoming hopelessly addicted. What is described in the following pages could be described as a parent and child's worst nightmare. Back then, before I learned all the things I earned in Nar-Anon/ Al-Anon (primarily that I, as well as Ryan, are "powerless" over his addiction), I started writing this as a way to help other parents and their kids learn from my mistakes and education through hard knocks. I thought I had learned why some of these things had happened and could advise others on how to avoid our plight.

So, I left the first part of this as I wrote it then, so the reader can see the metamorphosis I went through in learning about addiction, its causes and cures. What I have learned since is what they call in these programs the "3 C's: You didn't cause it; you can't control it; and you can't cure it! What you can do is learn to cope with it so it doesn't ruin your life as well.

CHAPTER 1

THE PICK-UP

The beige Toyota Camry pulled slowly up in front of the house. Two of the largest men I've ever seen stepped out. The first guy, Tom, a former policeman –turned- parole officer, was soft-spoken.

"Is Ryan here yet?" he asked calmly.

"Not yet", I said, although, just seconds later, his silver Hyundai Tiburon pulled into the driveway. Ryan and his friend, Mike, slowly exited the car. They looked over toward us, then walked into the house, glancing nervously back at us.

It was 1:00 AM Sunday morning. Ryan and Mike were just returning for a "sleepover", after, undoubtedly, another night out partying.

Ben, the second big man to emerge from the Toyota, was easily more than 260 pounds, and in his mid-30s.

"Well", Ben said, "It would have been easier if he was alone, but we've dealt with this before".

We all walked to the front door of the house I had lived in but left several months before when all our lives were coming apart. As we entered, a startled-looking Ryan was standing in the living room with Mike.

"What's going on?" he demanded.

Tom immediately took charge.

"Mike, you need to go outside NOW! We need to talk to Ryan."

Mike's face went ashen, as he muttered "fine".

"Ryan, please step into the bedroom, now" Tom ordered.

Ryan quickly complied, looking a little scared.

"What have I done? What's this about", he asked with a frightened tone.

My heart went out to him. Ryan still was, despite having just turned 17, that "scared little boy" I had been told by his psychologist was still inside him despite his tough exterior manner.

Ryan's mother (my then estranged wife) and I had been told that we would have a chance to say goodbye to him, once they got him in the car. They also said that, should he become verbally abusive, they would just drive away.

Several minutes later, these very large men escorted my only son out of the bedroom, and walked him slowly out of the house to the Toyota still parked in the driveway. As he looked at us with a look of bewilderment, Ryan declared, "You are making a big mistake!"

As Tom helped him rather forcefully into the waiting car and closed the door, Ryan's eyes were burning a hole through me. The men locked the door and rolled the window down about 5 inches.

I looked at him sadly through the window. "I love you, son", I said choking on tears. "I'm doing this for your own good".

"You will never see me again!" Ryan shouted at me. "I'm turning to an f..king life of crime".

The Toyota immediately went into reverse, as I watched them drive away with my son. It was the last time I would see him for almost six months.

I walked back into the house, in a state of shock. Not knowing what to do or say at that moment, but feeling the need to do something, I approached my soon-to-be-ex-wife and said "is there anything you'd like to talk about?"

"I have nothing to say to you", she barked. I knew then that, despite her agreement that this needed to be done, she was blaming me for the decision to send our son away.

Not knowing what else to do, I slowly left the house and climbed into my car. As I began to break down emotionally my mind wandered back to happier times with my little boy as he was growing up: Christmases, trips to Grandma's house, vacations to Florida, just us playing together when he was young.

Where had I gone wrong? What brought us to this turning point where I felt no choice but to send my only child, just one week past his 17th birthday, 500 miles away to a disciplinary boarding school for the next year? I might not see or talk to him for 4 to 6 months.

What went wrong? This is my story of what brought us to this point of no return.....

CHAPTER 2

THE CHILD WHO ALMOST WASN'T

Let me first start by saying clearly that the opinions I am about to express are just that, my opinions. I am no child psychologist, and certainly no expert on child-rearing. I have made more than my share of mistakes. I am only a father trying desperately to understand what went awry in my child's life and learn from it.

Some of what you will read may sound as if I am "bashing" my ex-wife. This is not my intent. I am just trying to factually relate what I observed, from my own vantage point. Believe me, I made more than my share of critical mistakes along the way, and developed a pattern of placating both of them to try to make them happy, get some peace and quiet, or try in the wrong way to express love and caring. As a result of what I experienced, I would like to express some ideas that might help others avoid the same plight. Therefore, for what they are worth, I am inserting, throughout the book, lessons I have learned along the way about fatherhood and marriage. They are simply opinions.

When I say I am trying to help "others", I mean primarily children, who are born totally innocent. They have no choice of who their parents are. We choose that for them, and it's an important and critical choice we make. I have had many months to reflect on this, and it is my firm belief that the desire to have children, and to love them, is a fundamental one in picking a spouse. I also have concluded very strongly, that not all people should be parents. Just because you can be a parent, does not mean you should be.

My advice to anyone considering marriage is this. Please, for the benefit of unborn children, make sure your prospective husband or wife (assuming you want children, and I did), has the same burning desire for kids that you do. Also, consider the mental health of the person you are planning to partner with. Is he or she up to the rigors of being a parent? Rearing a child is not, as they say, for the faint-hearted! Please also understand that you cannot change someone else, or rescue them from their problems or personal issues. In short, you cannot make someone else happy if they are not

When I met, and was dating, the woman I eventually married; there was little discussion on the issue of children. When the topic did come up, Melinda simply told me she already had a daughter (from her first, very brief, marriage) and that having another child was not a priority for her (kind of a "been there, done that" sort of thing). All I can say now, in painful retrospect is that this should have been the first "red flag" for me that perhaps I was with the wrong person.

I came from a large family, was accustomed to having a lot of brothers and sisters, and really wanted children. To me this was a loving and happy environment. Melinda, on the other hand, was an only child, and seemed to feel that "one was enough". (This was a subtle hint, but there was more, much more to come). She told me on many occasions that she was a "loner" in spirit, and did not feel comfortable being frequently around other people. As just one example, she often felt very uncomfortable being around my very large, extended family.

Another serious issue in the life of my first wife was the fact that she was chronically unhappy, depressed and weary. She was constantly tired, always said she felt bad, and just in general seemed to never be happy. I constantly heard, throughout our life together things like "I'm so depressed", and "I hate my life". All of this was despite the fact that she had no evident reason for these feelings. It seemed as if she was also constantly physically sick, to the point where I concluded a lot of it was psychosomatic. When I say this, I do not mean to imply that she was not really sick. She obviously was. What I mean is that her expectation of becoming sick and feeling bad made it happen for real. I'm a firm believer that choosing the wrong thoughts will make your worst fears come true!

I have had enough time to reflect on this and the problems of my child and my response to them to conclude that another pattern of mine is my need on some level to be a "rescuer" of others. As a result, I, and perhaps many of you, believed I could change another person for the better. I also had this ridiculous idea (in hindsight), that I could "rescue" her and make her happy. I thought she would start seeing the world the way I did. I believed I was such a good and happy person that I could fill the "voids" that another person felt inside. Have any of you ever believed this? I am here to tell you now that this will not happen!

In my case, I ignored the first obvious red flag, thinking to myself "she'll come around". I did tell her, after we had become married, that I always wanted a child (actually several). I also remember saying, "just because you have had one and are satisfied with that, should not mean I do not get to experience this joy in my life". This did not seem to matter to her (another red flag-my fundamental lifetime desires were inconsequential to her).

The topic did come up more frequently after we were married. When she was no longer able to deflect it with "it's not a priority to me", she became more assertive.

"I'm not cut out to be a mother", she would say, "I am not good at it. I don't enjoy it. Besides, I've already had a child."

My response grew steadily more frustrated in tone. "I'm glad you are satisfied with that, but I'm not. I've always wanted a child of my own", I would say.

Over the next 5 years, this conversation happened more and more frequently. In the ultimate hindsight, my persuasiveness and persistence, and ability to "guilt trip" her won out. What a mistake, in retrospect. If you find yourself in this situation, please don't do what I did. For the sake of your unborn child, move on. Start over!

The 9 months of her pregnancy with Ryan were some of the worst months of her (and my) life, and time we spent together. She was miserable being pregnant. It was a very hot summer and our house did not, at that time in our lives, have central air conditioning. She did not see pregnancy and an expectation of bringing new life into the world as a joy or a special gift, as some women do. I think the entire pregnancy experience served to heighten her sense of resentment about motherhood, and the fact that I had pressured her into it.

Ryan came into the world at 5:00 am on September 27, 1988. I was there to witness his birth and, up until that day, it was the greatest, happiest day of my life. I was the first person to hold him, and tears were streaming down my cheeks. What an experience it is to see your child born, and hold him. I highly recommend this experience to anyone who hasn't had it (that is, provided you want a child, I mean really, really want one, like I did!) How could I have known at this point what the future would hold?

Another obvious area of mismatch was the fact that my ex-wife, whatever her upbringing and rearing had taught her about religion and spirituality, was not even close to being on the same page with me. I had attended church every week growing up and my faith was important to me. Melinda, on the other hand, while saying she was a believer, did not see value in religious practice. Even worse, both for our marriage and future child-rearing, she avoided church services even when I was, in later years, trying to impress upon Ryan how important spirituality is to a happy, centered life.

As will be discussed later, Melinda also "blamed God" for her many perceived problems in life, from her depression and unhappiness, to events that occurred that she saw as evidence that God was not a "loving God". For example, many years later, her daughter bore a child who was born with a handicap. Melinda always saw this as a curse. "Why did God do this to us?" she would ask continually.

I can only say that, to the detriment of my only son, I prevailed upon the wrong woman to become his mother. As the rest of my story will demonstrate, I learned, very painfully, the most enduring lesson a person can learn. If you learn nothing else from my story, please glean this: You cannot make a mother of someone who does not really want to be one, and is not "cut out" for it!

Anyone can bear a child. Only someone who truly wants and loves children can be a good mom. I have also learned that a person must be happy and well-adjusted to be well prepared for parenthood. Please don't make the mistake of believing you can cure "defects" in another human being. For the sake of your unborn child, if you really want one, and want the child's happiness, find someone who desperately wants to be a mother (or father). This is fundamental to the future of a child, and even to a happy marriage!

CHAPTER 3

SLEEPLESS NIGHTS

From the time Ryan was a baby, even from the very first day we brought him home from Mt Carmel hospital in Columbus, it was obvious to me that motherhood presented serious problems for his mom. I think this situation really, seriously "upset her apple cart". Ryan had difficulty sleeping through the night and woke up every 3 hours wanting to eat. He was a larger than average baby (10 pounds at birth) and was always hungry! Although many babies present these types of challenges for their parents, I think the reaction of his mom was atypical.

Being awakened every 3 hours for the first month or more was almost more than she could handle. He cried a lot, and so did she. Many times I thought she was on the verge of some type of mental breakdown. (I think children can definitely read this in the way they are talked to and held). I frequently heard "I don't think I can handle this", and, at the first opportunity she started giving Ryan some semi-solid baby cereal in his bottle to encourage him to sleep longer.

As a "rescuer", I stepped in and did all I could to relieve her of this burden. Many times I did more than my share of getting up in the night and feeding him. As mentioned, we always used bottles. She was very firm in her refusal to even consider breast feeding. The whole idea of this seriously "grossed her out"! Despite the relief I tried to give her, it was not enough. She was still awake and crying, and "feeling like a zombie". The stress this put on our relationship and upon her ability to "bond" with her son was severely affected.

The more of this I witnessed, the more determined I became to basically fill the "mothering" role and ensure that my son got the love I felt he was lacking. I doted over him, and did much more than I should have done to placate him and make him happy. I did this both to supply love that I felt was lacking for him, as well as to keep him from bothering his mother, frankly, so I didn't have to listen to her constant complaining.

As I will describe later in the book, this began a pattern, almost from the outset of Ryan's life, of his being placated, not permitted to experience boredom where he could bother his mother, and our caving in to almost any demand or desire he had. (My own Dad told me many years later, that his Grandson Ryan's biggest problem was that he never heard the word "no", and never learned to accept it!) I confess at this point to being just as guilty of this as she was, under the perverse notion that I was showing him love, and keeping him from getting on his mother's always-frayed nerves.

Another important lesson I learned was my second biggest mistake. Children need discipline, boundaries and consequences to learn appropriate behaviors and to grow up well adjusted. Saying "yes" to them all the time does not mean you are loving. Sometimes saying "no" is the best experience for them in the long run and is the most important thing you can say to a loved one who is relying on you to teach them.

It is also very important that children be given and taught to take on responsibilities. This starts around the house. Ryan was basically never given any significant responsibility and things we did ask of him we stepped in and did ourselves when he refused to do them, or just ignored our requests. He therefore learned that responsibilities are just requests and not real. If you ignore them, they will go away.

CHAPTER 4

A CONFUSED LITTLE BOY

From the time Ryan was a very young child, I believe his upbringing was confusing to him. His mother stayed at home with him, ostensibly to provide a good home environment for him. I was working for a large insurance company and able to provide a pretty good income to the family. While at first blush this sounds like a great way to raise a child, this was not a "June and Ward Cleaver" style home or environment. I traveled frequently for my job, and Melinda, in my opinion, did not really want to be bothered with raising a child.

From the youngest of ages, my son got to watch a lot of television (a surrogate babysitter) and, I believe, learned that he was not supposed to bother his mom too much. What I witnessed when I was around was a mother who tried to figure out ways to occupy Ryan, without having to spend too much time interacting with him. This took the form of television, video games at an early age, and buying a lot of toys and material things to keep him busy (more on this in later chapters).

Ryan, also, was somewhat difficult. He was dubbed "Cryin' Ryan" by one of his sister Charity's friends. As described earlier, Ryan learned that all he had to do was cry or throw a fit and he got something to placate him, and hopefully, keep him quiet. I believe he was taught this behavior and was 25 years old before he learned to break out of it. He never learned, as most kids do when they move from baby to adolescence, that crying or bad behavior was not an appropriate form of expression. Instead, he learned that there would be some reward or at least a reaction to it. Moreover, I think his mother also demonstrated this same immature behavior. And I not only tolerated it, but placated her as well. This only cemented the learning in Ryan's mind.

While my reaction to this behavior was tolerance and placating, Melinda's reaction to him was far from a loving one. It did not lead to personal, positive interaction or teaching appropriate responses. Instead, he was scolded, or criticized, then usually given a toy or movie to keep him quiet.

One of Melinda's favorite activities was to go out to dinner on Friday nights. Ryan, as a young child, could not be left at home and babysitters were not frequently available. He gained experience very early on at going out to restaurants. He also learned, however, that if he disrupted our conversation, he would get a reward. His mother enjoyed this ritual (one of the few things she enjoyed) because of the opportunity for adult conversation. "I'm stuck all day with a toddler; I need someone to talk to".

When Ryan tried to get attention, he would act out, throw things around, or cry. Very quickly he learned that he would receive a new toy, such as a Lego, every Friday night to keep him occupied so he would not disrupt the conversation. If we went to dinner 50 Friday nights a year, Ryan probably got 50 new toys a year! What this taught him was that if you behave inappropriately, there will be efforts made to keep you quiet or reward you with something new!

When he was at home with her, he could do nothing right. He and I both experienced a great deal of criticism for some of the most minor things you could imagine.(I used to get yelled at for making fingerprints on the stainless steel refrigerator door). The good news for me was that I had grown up in a happy home and had learned a positive self esteem. Ryan would tell me many years later, that he was criticized to such a degree that he believed he could do nothing right, so he might as well be bad! After all, this is what was expected of him. (I frequently heard her say to him "what's wrong with you?") Instead of attacking or commenting upon behavior that was inappropriate, she attacked the person.

We also moved a lot. From the time Ryan was born, until he was in junior high school, we lived in 4 different houses, and he went to 5 different schools. Every home we bought "got old" to Melinda after about 2 years, and she wanted something bigger and nicer. In my efforts to placate her and hopefully keep her happy,(shut her up), I went along. In the most recent house we owned together, we spent $50,000 to totally gut and remodel a kitchen that most people in our income range would have thought was fine "as is".

It's probably a good time now to address the obvious questions in your mind "why would you agree to all this", or "why did you let her get away with all that?" These are obviously very good questions that I have had to contemplate for a long time. I have concluded that there were a couple reasons. First, as mentioned already, I was a rescuer. I kept feeling and hoping that giving her what she wanted would eventually make her happy. (You get what you want, how can you be unhappy, right? WRONG!) Also, her reactions to not getting what she wanted were so extreme, that I learned I didn't want to be exposed to it. She would cry, mope, not talk, complain, whine, and generally make those around her miserable. When I learned to do this with her, it was easily translated into taking the same approach with Ryan, who quickly (and already) learned the same behaviors.

Vacations were similar to houses. Every year we had to take an expensive vacation, sometimes spending $4,000-$5,000 on each trip. It always had to be to one of the nicest, most expensive resorts we could find. Meals had to be eaten out and dinners were generally $100-150 per day. Often times we went into debt to pay for these amenities. Most times, on most trips (yes, I did say "most", easily approaching 90% of the time) we would have to change hotel rooms, because the first one wasn't big enough, clean enough, or fancy enough, for Melinda. Sometimes we would change hotels altogether. On some occasions we would end up spending twice as much as planned prior to the trip!

Furthermore, whenever any type of conflict arose (as in any family, but I believe more frequently in our case), Ryan would be told, "you ruined my trip"! My son not only witnessed this, but was a target of it. I believe he learned a lot from it. When his mother threw an emotional fit because the hotel or room was not "just right", I agreed to change it.

Knowing her as I did, I knew that our vacation would have no peace if I did not go along with the ridiculous demand to move. I wanted to try to make her happy, and I wanted some peace. What a lesson to learn the hard way.

What my son learned from witnessing all this was that it was not only appropriate to throw an emotional fit if you were unhappy, it served to get you something nicer and better in return!

CHAPTER 5

STORM WARNINGS!

When Ryan was probably as young as 8 or 9, I started to see increasing signs of impending trouble on the horizon. As described earlier, in order to placate him and keep him quiet, he watched a lot of television and movies. From a very early age, he was watching shows that depicted, in my opinion, too much violence and troubling images. The shows contained much-too-mature subject matter for him at just about every age. (This would later be true of video games he played, and wanted). I have to equally blame myself here. Whatever he wanted, I pretty much gave in to, to keep him happy, and avoid conflict, which was so frequent in our dysfunctional home. This became a vicious cycle of increasing demands, more bad behavior, more placating.

Here's where my role was critical in Ryan's eventual downfall. I should have asserted myself more, both in discipline and in just plain providing guidance for him in many areas of his life. I was gone frequently on business. When I was home, I would hear from Ryan about how his mother "treats me like crap", describing constant criticism and ill treatment. I can honestly say that I rarely, if ever, observed loving interaction between them. There was a lot of hollering, yelling and fighting.

Soon both of them began to complain to me of the other's treatment. They both would use identical terminology "She (or he) treats me like crap"! Ryan confided to me one time that it made him sad to go to his friends houses to play because he got to see how kind and nice the other kid's mothers were, and that "I have to have a mother like this. Why can't I have a nice mother"? This tugged at my heart strings in a major way. So, I continued placating him and his mother, trying to keep the peace, and giving in to both of their demands. These grew in frequency, intensity and irrationality. It got to the point that I did not know whom and how much to believe. Both accounts of every conflict were self-serving and designed to get me to "take sides" with the person recounting the event.

Ryan, at around age 10 or 11, started to become interested in violent and incendiary things. He once threw a hatchet at a neighbor boy's foot during a disagreement, and we got a very concerned call from the boy's mother. Ryan also developed an intense interest in fire and fireworks. He and a neighbor boy in junior high put fire crackers in a hole in the ground and blew a bigger hole.

Ryan also had trouble adjusting to his mother's frequent need to change environments. The neighbor kids at one of our many house moves just did not accept him, and he had frequent run-ins with these kids on the school bus. We had many conversations with other parents about his behavior, even while Ryan was telling us he was the victim. It got so bad in one of the neighborhoods, that we first put him in a private school, then later moved again.

A year or so later was Ryan's first involvement with the police. We had just moved for the 3rd time in Ryan's short life, when we got a call that he and several kids were found at a picnic table in the park with a gasoline can and some matches. The police brought him home, but no charges were filed. They did discuss with us the fact that when kids get involved with fire, it should be taken as a warning sign of some emotional disturbance. In their experience, these kids often had other more serious emotional things going on within them. Although we discussed taking him to a psychologist, we were "in denial" and did not act upon this advice. Shortly thereafter, Ryan began to acquire lighters and lighter fluid. He sprayed aerosol cans, and placed lighters in front of them to make a make-shift flame-thrower (one time inside the house).

Ryan then began to acquire knives and became interested in weapons. The day he got out of 8th grade (his second involvement with the law), he and a couple friends threw some gasoline in a portable toilet near his junior high school and dropped in a lit match. The toilet and the one beside it both caught fire and melted. We ended up paying about $2,000 in restitution for the damage he caused. The more embarrassing aspect of this for me as a parent, and another example of my serious mistakes in child-rearing, is that there were never any serious consequences for Ryan as a result of this behavior. I always bailed him out, paid for his mistakes, and placated him. (I guess I thought this was showing him that he really was "loved"!)

When Ryan was in 7th and 8th grade, his behavior became, to me, even more bizarre. In addition to violent and strange movies that he wanted to watch, he began listening to music that glorified violence and hopelessness. (System of a Down's, *Toxicity*, was one of his favorite songs, and he told me he agreed with the lyrics.) He also began dressing in black, and wanting all-black clothes. He described himself as "Goth" and wanted a black cloak. He said he wanted to dress in dark clothing, because it matched the way he felt, "dark inside". I permitted this for awhile, thinking it was a phase he was going through.

Also about this time was when he began refusing to go to church with me, and cancelled his scheduled acolyte duties. He announced he did not believe in God, and thought religious teachings were stupid. I mentioned that this was another area in which his mom and I were not on the same page, to Ryan's detriment. She, too, would usually be disinterested in church services, or downright hostile to them. When her daughter, gave birth to a child with cerebral palsy, Melinda blamed God for "doing this to her". Ryan also said things like, "if there is a God, he's screwing with my life!"

I will now interject what should be obvious to the reader. Don't be afraid to defy the "experts" who say media images and music lyrics can't affect behavior. Don't be afraid to monitor and censor your kids' TV, movies, music and internet use. If you think religious training is important, don't be afraid to "force it" a little!

Ryan became increasingly disrespectful to us as his parents and in his use of fowl language. Whenever he wanted to do something, for example, dress in the black cloak and wear it to school, we were in for a cursing tirade anytime we told him "no" on this or anything else. My pattern of giving in continued, and I avoided telling him "no", except in the worst extremes of his behavior, again to avoid the tirade and keep the peace. By this time I was getting phone calls on business trips from both Ryan and his mom, telling me continually that the other was "treating me like crap".

Ryan then also began using the phrases "I hate my life" and "I'm so depressed". I asked his mother "where did he learn that?" He began to talk of suicide, and hating his life enough to end it. He carved on his own skin with a knife, the word "forsaken" on his arm in his own blood!

Increasingly, Melinda and I were in disagreement over how to handle him, and he developed a manipulative approach to "divide and conquer" between the 2 of us. I became more convinced that her harsh approach in dealing with him was turning him on us. I continued my placating, "no consequences" approach to Ryan's discipline, hoping to counter-balance her, in my opinion, unnecessarily harsh and critical manner.

Moving into his high school years, Ryan's behavior became increasingly violent and out-of-control. He punched holes in the walls when he became angry, and swore at us frequently. Emotional outbursts and tirades became the norm, for both Ryan and his mom, while my pattern of "just keep the peace" became ingrained in my behavior. There were also physical altercations between the 2 of us.

CHAPTER 6

"WEED" IN THE CLOSET AND INTO THE ABYSS

In 2004, during his sophomore year in high school, Ryan began locking the door to his bedroom. He told me it was because the room was a mess; he needed to clean it up, and did not want to hear his mom give him a "load of crap" about how messy it was until he could clean it. "She screams at me every day about my room. I can't take it", he would say. Then in June, after school was out, we got a letter from a parent of one of Ryan's friends. The letter said this parent had been monitoring the e-mail correspondence of his son. His son had gotten a letter from Ryan claiming to have been "high 24/7 since school's been out", taking a variety of drugs.

We confronted Ryan with this information. A lot of angry words were exchanged, and we insisted upon his opening his room, so we could search it. After angry protests and swearing, we got the room open and discovered 7 or 8 marijuana plants growing under a heat light in Ryan's closet. These were perhaps 12 to 14 inches in height, so they had been growing awhile. When confronted with this, Ryan denied taking the drugs himself, saying he was growing it for a friend and he did it to "make some money". Disbelieving this story, we immediately grounded Ryan and insisted he start seeing a psychologist. We also told him that, even if the story were true, selling drugs was an even more serious offense.

CHAPTER 7

THE CAR

At this point, what I am about to tell you will strain your ability to keep from concluding that I was not only a totally indulgent father, but perhaps totally crazy as well. (As I later found out in Al-Anon, I was definitely "living the insanity" as is described in the 12 steps). Anyway, when Ryan turned 16, I rushed out and bought him a car. We had been talking about it for a year or so, and his insistence led me to live up to what I at the time described as a "commitment" to him and spent $10,000 on a 1997 Hyundai Tiburon. Ryan was ecstatic with the car, and it immediately led to his having even more dangerous "freedom" than before.

It wasn't very long until the car was found, in the middle of the night on top of a small hill, perhaps 40 feet off the street, and I got up in the night to meet the tow truck. There was significant damage to the car. Ryan had been driving too fast around a curve on a residential street near our home and had totally left the road in some snow. What did I do? I paid a couple thousand dollars to have the car repaired. Did Ryan receive any real consequences for his actions? (Like loss of driving privileges or grounding or anything of that nature?) No.

I recall one completely insane night very vividly. Ryan was calling me on his cell phone, telling me he was driving down the road by the river, looking for a place to drive his car into the water, intending to kill himself. I was driving around trying to find him and stop him. Why was he doing this? He said he was "so depressed" and "hated his life" and wanted to end it.

This was just the beginning of situations involving this car, from being caught with drug paraphernalia, stopped with a carload of friends doing pot, as well as several other accidents, ruined tires and the like. By this time, you probably will not be surprised to learn that I spent almost the entire value of the original purchase price of this car repairing it for damage that went well beyond "normal wear and tear". Eventually, as will be dealt with in other chapters of this book, I finally did stop repairing the car, as the damage Ryan inflicted upon it in his drug-induced states became more and more serious, and the car became a rolling wreck. (It eventually was totaled in an accident Ryan walked away from and nobody else was hurt, thank God!)

In reflecting back on the car, the decisions I made about it, and my "inability", (I will now call it) to impose any significant discipline, has given me many, many sleepless nights and discussions with Al-Anon and Nar-Anon friends trying to figure out "why" I did what I did. I have heard some parents with similar kids say, in describing their decision making and "enabling" that they were afraid their child was going to die. I guess I felt that way as well. But, perhaps even more importantly, I had been through so many "temper tantrums" with Ryan as a teenager, that I actually became conditioned to do what he was asking to try to get some peace and not have the inevitable fight that would ensue whenever he didn't get his own way. I had this same pattern with my wife, who also was very emotional, and difficult to reason with. She was chronically unhappy and I found myself giving in to her to keep the peace.

In short, I was a complete "coward" in both of these relationships. I wondered what was wrong with Ryan. All I had to do was look in the mirror!

CHAPTER 8

TO "INSANITY AND BEYOND"

To fast forward from there, things began to deteriorate even more rapidly in all of our lives. This time period is like a blur in my life, and the immense negativity of it all, and emotional burden, makes it impossible to remember the exact sequence of events. Ryan was arrested multiple times on curfew violations, drug possession and paraphernalia charges, theft charges, speeding tickets and the like. He was also charged with obstructing justice for fleeing the police, and domestic violence for threatening his mother. These were all juvenile charges. I spent probably $6,000 on attorneys to represent him. When he went away he was on probation for 13 criminal, juvenile charges. He spent a weekend in the juvenile detention facility for the domestic violence charge.

His grades in school also began to take a serious slide. We had multiple meetings with counselors and teachers. Ryan's excuses were things like. "the math teacher's an A..Hole. He doesn't like me", and similar stories. It was never his fault.

I do remember many, many events that transpired over the next couple years; I just struggle with the order in which they occurred. One time, he broke a beer bottle on the counter top in the kitchen and threatened to slit my throat with it, then to slit his own throat. Several times he pushed me physically, threatened me, and wanted to start fights. He punched me and sometimes I would engage in physical altercations with him. I am not proud of this. When your child is that out of control, sometimes you just don't know what to do and you lose control yourself.

Ryan also spent a month, in early 2005, in a very fine and well-known substance abuse rehabilitation facility in Minnesota called Hazelden. It was one of the best programs of its kind in the nation. He never really bought into it. He at first refused to go, and then agreed only because it would look good to the court where his charges were pending. He even told me "This won't change me. I'll be just the same when I get out". His prediction was accurate.

During these same months Ryan's friends all changed. The kids he was hanging out with in 7th, 8th and 9th grades were all out of the picture. His new friends now were all drug abusers. We tried keeping him from seeing certain of his friends. This only worked for awhile. We ended up spying on him, following him, searching the house and his bedroom. The whole thing was a nightmare. Nothing seemed to help. Not the psychologists, not the arrests and court appearances.

Ryan seemed to have learned the lessons we taught him extremely well; if you throw a big enough fit and make those around you feel annoyed, threatened or scared; you will get a positive outcome. The first time this failed to work was when he told a police officer, after one arrest, that he might as well take his life, since his parents would probably kill him for being arrested again. The police took this as a suicide threat, and escorted him to Ohio State University's Psychiatric Hospital. They kept him there for a week for observation, and it was hard for us to get him out!

During this same time period, Ryan was frequently sneaking out to go party with friends, staying out all night, then sleeping through school the next day. If anyone tried to wake him up he would become verbally abusive and threaten to hurt whoever was unfortunate enough to try to wake him. The consequence of all this was that he failed most of his courses his junior year and was approximately a year behind at the point I made the tough decision to send him away.

While he was missing school and failing, he had his first of many court appearances on his charges. The juvenile court magistrate looked

Ryan right in the eye and said "if you don't start attending school, I will lock your ass up!" What do you think happened as a result of this? Ryan still didn't get it, and was still refusing to go to school. "I'm so far behind, what's the use", he would say. He also complained of having a stigma with all the teachers and other students. He also said it was too embarrassing to go to school.

After his final disposition with the court, where he entered guilty pleas to a couple charges, and others were dropped, he was put on probation for a year. One of the conditions of probation was attending school. The probation officer was very direct: "go to school or I will send you to jail or remove you from your home to a foster home or juvenile inpatient treatment center". Still Ryan continued to miss school on 3 or 4 days out of each week!

In early 2005, I made the difficult decision to leave my wife and start over. Our lives together had become unbearable. I sought help from the same psychologist Ryan was seeing who knew all about our family life. He confirmed some of my thinking, not only about Ryan but about Melinda and why I probably would never be happy staying with her. Some of it I have described in this book. There is really no point in dwelling on it. My main reasons for staying as long as I did in my unhappy, unloving marriage were basically 2 things: an inherent belief that kids are better off in an intact family (all other things being equal, that is), and my religious beliefs about the commitment you make before God in entering into a marriage, Suffice it to say, both of these were very powerful and meaningful to me. It just became crystal clear to me that there was nothing saving Ryan in this particular "intact family".

I concluded he and I would be better off getting out from under the same roof with his mother. However, Ryan did not cooperate. All of his friends were still living in the same suburb where our house was, and his school (though he was refusing to attend) was there. He stayed and I left, while trying to encourage him to join me. He made his mom's life miserable, and would only see me when he needed money, which, I am sad to say, I continued to give him a couple times a week.

He made me feel guilty every time I tried to cut him off (which happened several times). His manipulation would go something like this: "Dad, you abandoned me here in misery with mom. The least you can do is give me some money so I can go somewhere and do something fun with my friends. All of these problems are because of the stress I'm feeling over you and mom splitting up"! Obviously he would not listen when I pointed out that he was having most of these or similar problems long before I decided to leave!

In late summer of 2005, after school was out, Ryan was enrolled in 2 home study courses to try to catch up. He wasn't doing the work on these, either. He was obviously still taking drugs and staying up all night. In my conversations with the psychologist, he was insistent that something had to be done, or he felt we could lose Ryan. Still I didn't act. I did however, ask the psychologist for some ideas on where we might send Ryan for help, and he gave me a couple ideas of programs that might be good. I also started researching the internet for schools that specialized in discipline problems, and drug and alcohol abuse. I felt strongly that when and if I did something, it should be a program to instill some discipline that I, sorry to say, had never instilled in my son.

One particularly difficult issue for me happened in early October of 2005. My father passed away from colon cancer at age 73. Not only was Ryan pretty much absent throughout his illness, surgery and hospitalization (I think he went once to see his grandfather in the hospital), he could not even get himself out of bed to attend his funeral. This deeply saddened me, but also pointed out just what depths Ryan had sunk to in allowing these drugs and his now-adopted lifestyle to control him. This was a huge wake-up call to me that he would not be able to extricate himself from the abyss he had sunk into!

CHAPTER 9

THE POINT OF NO RETURN

What was the last straw? What was the breaking point? About 2 weeks before Ryan's 17th birthday in September of 2005, I convinced him to get together for dinner with me. I had been calling him every day wanting to see him and mostly he just refused to answer the phone and would not return my calls. This day he did. When we were returning to the house where he was staying with his mom, it was fairly late in the evening, around 11:00 pm or midnight. Ryan just emotionally melted down.

He started at first crying, and then got extremely angry. He complained about his mom and her treatment of him. He complained about my "leaving him", about school, and about his problems with the police and court system, and about his life in general. He said he hated his life, wanted to die, and hated the police for picking on him, distrusting him, following his car and harassing him. It was a very long conversation, and he didn't want me to leave. I honestly thought he might try to take his own life. By this time he was frequently threatening suicide.

Then, unexpectedly, he started into a tirade on how much he hated his car, and it was a piece of junk because the radio wasn't working all the time. He ripped the antennae off the car and threw it in the street, swearing, cursing and yelling loud enough for neighbors to hear.

"You'd better keep it down", I told him. "Somebody will call the police".

"F..k the police", he yelled, "If they come here, I'll kill the police".

Just about 5 minutes later, a police cruiser pulled in the driveway and 2 police officers got out. They questioned both of us about what the disturbance was all about.

One of the men said sharply to Ryan, "Did you say you would kill the police?"

"No", Ryan lied, "I was just hollering. I'm upset"

"Do you have any weapons or guns in the house", the officer demanded.

I assured the policeman we did not.

"You need to do something about him", the officer then told me pointedly. "He's out of control. We are tired of coming over here and having to deal with him. If you don't do something, we will. Maybe you should consider one of those disciplinary boarding schools to straighten him out", he said. "If not, he's going to end up locked up."

As I drove home to my newly-purchased condo that night, I was in deep reflection. The policeman was right, and I had been in denial. Something indeed had to be done. This situation was not going to rectify itself, I had to take decisive action, and there was not time to lose.

The only thing I had to lose was my son…

CHAPTER 10

MIDWEST ACADEMY

After being picked up early on that October Sunday morning, the 2 very large men drove my child through the night, on their way to a small town called Keokuk, Iowa. Keokuk is at the confluence of the Des Moines and Mississippi Rivers, and is the home of a boarding school called Midwest Academy. It is miles from any towns or cities of any size. Midwest is a school specializing in the handling of kids like Ryan, with disciplinary, drug/alcohol and legal problems. Most of the kids at Midwest have histories similar to my son's.

The men indicated that they would call me in the morning, and give me an update on their progress and how Ryan was faring on the trip. I heard from them around 8:00 am Monday morning as they neared the Midwest facility, about a 9 hour drive from our home in Columbus, Ohio. When I got the call, I was informed that Ryan was polite and slept most of the way. Despite his threats to me before that fateful night that I would "never get him to a boarding school alive", he made it there safely.

The escort guys said that he was likely "high" on something and slept most of the way. They speculated that he was on "meth", which Ryan later vehemently denied. (He did, however, admit to having used a combination of alcohol, marijuana, mushrooms and acid, prior to being picked up that night.)

INITIAL REACTION

At Midwest, the first thing they do is place the newly arrived kids in an observation lock-up to make sure they come down off anything they might be on and get "dried out". This lasts 24-48 hours and they are confined to a very small room, with no furniture or toilets. Although it sounded like a punitive placement, I was assured that they are observed, kept safe, and are well treated. Ryan's first letter to me was handwritten, and disputed this assurance:

"Dear Dad,

Hey, it's the first day of this hell-hole you think is going to help me. I understand why you are doing this, you think this is the only way you can "Save" my life. I know that you and mom love me, but please reconsider this decision. This place is dirty and disgusting. I was made to drive 10 hours through the night, where I was then put into a small (7",7",10") pine box. The food is terrible, people are cruel, and I was made to go to the bathroom in the corner because they wouldn't let me go to the bathroom. (I S—t on the floor, while locked for 24 hours in a small enclosure.) I can't stop crying dad, this is the absolute death of all I knew. Please reconsider for a moment that maybe you over-reacted a little. Bring me home immediately, I Beg You......"

Gut wrenching stuff! I began to tear up reading this, and nearly did begin to reconsider my decision. I sucked it up, however, said a prayer and realized that Ryan was on the verge of self-annihilation. I spoke to a "family rep" at the school, who told me that, early in the commitment of one of their new students, it is not uncommon to hear derogatory things about the school, the food, their treatment, etc. They reminded me that these kids are good manipulators, and would try to tug at your heart strings to get out and go back to the lives they had before.

As you might imagine, I was pretty much a basket case myself for the first couple weeks. I had been told that in this program, there would be no contact with my son, even by telephone for several months. The program has strict rules of discipline, and that the kids have to earn the right to a phone call home, and later a personal visit, through "good behavior" points. There were also demerit points for not strictly following the rules. (What a shame that I had to spend, over the next year, approximately $40,000 to have this place do for my son what I never had the strength or perseverance to do on my own!)

I was impressed about what I had learned about the program. Kids go to school 6 days a week for 6 or 7 hours at a time, and can learn and advance at their own pace. Teaching and testing is done largely by computer, and I was assured that if Ryan applied himself like never before, he could complete 2 years of high school (he was almost a year behind) in one year. In addition, a student will not go on to the next task or test until and unless they get a least a B on each part of the course.

The kids are permitted (and actually required) to write home once per week, and Sunday is the designated writing day. If a parent has e-mail, they can receive these letters via e-mail. It is the preferred manner of communication with your kids. Parents can write as frequently as they wish, but the kids are limited to one outgoing letter per week.

Despite the despair expressed in his first letter, Ryan's second letter was quite the opposite. At the time I did not know if it expressed his real feelings or if it was designed to manipulate me to believe he was "fixed":

"10-26-2005

Dear Dad,

Hey....I don't really know what to say. I got your letter and I want you to know that I'm not angry with you. I understand why you did this and in a way, I'm glad you did. I wasn't getting it, you are absolutely right....I'm so sorry it had to come to this and I take full responsibility for my being here, (I put myself in this situation) I want you to know, I'm going to do everything I can to take full advantage of this place....I realize that under my own power, I would only have brought myself to destruction. I thank you for sending me here, you have really saved my life....."

I got very emotional again, reading this. I really wanted to believe him. I wanted desperately to know my son was finally "getting it" and that he knew it would be necessary to stay there awhile and make some pretty drastic life changes! For the time being, I had a feeling that he was at peace, protected and safe, and in a place where he had the opportunity to make some positive self-changes. As a result, I had the first peaceful night's sleep I had had in several years after receiving this letter.

The kids at Midwest are expected to attend (and pass) a series of seminars designed to reveal to them many aspects of themselves. It is a very valuable self-examination process, and parents are invited and encouraged to attend these seminars as well, separately (they do not attend with their children.) Ryan attended these, and after each one, reported to me in his weekly letter that they were, indeed, "life changing experiences". I was fortunate enough to attend 2 of them myself, in Chicago, and I can strongly support his statements about how very meaningful and potentially life-changing they are if you throw yourself into them and embrace them!

I was also fortunate to have my new friend and life partner (now my new wife, Karen) attend these seminars with me. Ryan's mother came up with excuses not to attend for many months. Then, after she did attend one seminar near the end of Ryan's stay at Midwest, declared it a "waste of time". Karen, anticipating playing a future role in Ryan's life, embraced the seminars and learned some valuable things about herself that she could apply in her own life and in rearing her own child.

HOLIDAY STRESS

The next mini-crises in Ryan's life occurred when he was sequestered at Midwest during the 2 big holidays of Thanksgiving and Christmas. The tone of his letters turned negative, particularly the one he wrote at Christmas time. He was understandably very down and feeling depressed at that time, and took the opportunity to unload on me for several things.

> "...I am very upset right now. In some ways I feel I'd rather be in the foster home or jail than be here. At least in those places I would still be able to have visits....I miss our Chritmases we used to have. It doesn't matter if there were problems, we were a family....I don't think I will ever be able to get past the pain I feel.... I am so depressed...."

On a brighter note, the following letter was very positive and apologetic, and admitted that he was just really "down" because of being away from home and family at Christmas.

> "...I just want to express how sorry I am for my last letter. I want you to know that none of that was how I really feel...I was angry and I was hurt. ...because of the greed and selfish lust for all the things I rightfully lost....the same day I wrote the letter, I went back and re-read it and felt terrible for all the things I said...."

I was encouraged that he was able to bounce back. Like so much of Ryan's life up until that point, the year at Midwest was an emotional "roller-coaster" with good days and bad days. As I later would learn when I started learning about myself in Nar-Anon, I was so totally absorbed in Ryan's life, I could not have a good day in my life if he were having a bad day.

Our First Visit- Unscheduled

In March of 2006, my brother, Steve, passed away from colon cancer at age 54. Because Ryan was away at Midwest, I had to get special permission to fly him home for the funeral. It was the first time I had been able to see him in 5 months. It was a tearful reunion for both of us when he came walking out of the concourse at the Dayton, Ohio airport. It was a bittersweet 24 hour period he was able to spend at home. I was extremely sad over the loss of my older brother, but happy to get to see Ryan after so many months. It was difficult to sort out these conflicting emotions for both of us.

On March 27, after getting back to school, Ryan wrote:

"...I wanted to tell you that the experience I had coming up (to Ohio) was really amazing and I believe a really good one for me. Just being able to talk to Grandma and the relatives and tell them what has been going on with me, gave me the biggest sense of belonging and closure. It has always been my worry to ever see them again, for fear I would be rejected on account of my past actions. I now have seen, and do know in full, my family will always be there for me, in good and bad. I am so sad for Uncle Steve's death, but at the same time am glad I had the opportunity to come home for awhile...."

The reference above to his "past actions", in addition to his legal and behavioral problems, also incorporated one single, biggest concern about facing my mom. This was Ryan's missing his Grandfather's funeral, which he knew was an extreme disappointment to much of the family, and a major factor in waking up all of us to the seriousness of Ryan's plight.

COMING TO GRIPS WITH MOM'S INFLUENCE

Soon after this letter, on April 3, he finally wrote a letter to his mother (which he sent to me and asked me to deliver to her, as she still had not gotten around to setting up an e-mail to assist in communications with her. I had left her a brand-new Dell desktop when I moved out). I had been receiving, weekly and like clockwork, a Sunday letter from Ryan that I always got on Mondays. He admitted that he had been avoiding writing to his mom, not knowing what to say to her. In this letter, some of his lifetime frustrations came out:

"Dear Mom,

Hi... I feel there are some things I need to let you know. I have been avoiding writing to you and dealing with some issues I have since I arrived at Midwest Academy. This has caused me a lot of problems and a lot of emotional turmoil. I am not avoiding anymore... I am tired of sugar-coating my feelings and experiences because I am afraid of hurting you. I haven't told you really what I feel because of this. I love you so much Mom and I want a relationship with you, but am afraid. I am afraid to write you and afraid to have a relationship with you because I never have had one before. You and I have never got along at all. I have so many dark memories in my life of you yelling at me and making me feel worthless. I have so many beliefs and feelings about myself that I am nothing and am not worth anything good in life. Every time you told me that I "ruined the vacation and we are going to go home". Every time you made me feel like crap, which was pretty much any time I was around you. I can't tell you how many issues and problems I have that I feel I am going to have to spend the rest of my life dealing with, that are because of you. I know I had a little part in these fights and yelling matches, but you were cruel to me Mom. All I ever wanted was to know inside that you loved me and I was good enough for you. That Charity wasn't your favorite and you actually wanted me as a son. I never felt like I was meant to be and always felt like you hated me. You have asked me that before and I have been afraid to tell you. I have never felt like you gave a damn about me. I always have felt like you hated me and regarded me as nothing more then the dirt beneath your feet. I am so afraid that you are going to just take this all as some sort of attack when that is not what I mean at all. These are feelings that I have been able to express to everyone else but you, since I have arrived. I just didn't want to hurt you. I know how much you are still holding onto this divorce thing and how much it hurts you. Well, I think you are comfortable in your pain mom..."

This letter was much longer, but the tone was mostly the same! When Ryan finally wrote to his mother for the first time, I had already received 25 weekly letters from him (48 in total in the 11 months he was there; almost exactly one per week).

Confession Time

Soon after this, in mid-April, I received a stunning letter from Ryan that I will reproduce in full below. I learned a lot from this letter, including many things that were totally frightening and new to me. His willingness to write this, I hoped, was the beginning of a "turnaround". This was the first attempt at a so-called "confession letter", that they are encouraged to write when they attend the seminars:

"Dear Parents,

I am addressing this to one and to you both at the same time. I know I have written a personal form of this letter to you, Dad, but it was "half-assed" and spur of the moment. Mom, honestly I have been avoiding writing this because it is so awkward for me. I also didn't want to hurt you. So without further avoidance here is my Confession Letter, of all I did and participated in that contributed to my downfall as a person. I send this letter in faith that it will be understood that I only want the best relationship I can have with you both and want to have a "clean slate", so to speak. So here it is…

First of all I am going to start with drugs. My first experience with drugs was in 9th grade. I used to sneak out at night and go over to James Seelbach's house in the middle of the night. We used to hang out and talk about all the things in the world that were stupid and wrong. I would consider both him and I in the "gothic" clique of middle school during this time and we were both pretty dark and depressed. We used to read out of the satanic bible and play with fire and gasoline. My first experience with drugs was there when I tried some cherry brandy at his house. It tasted pretty good and was honestly my first experience getting drunk. During this time in my life I was rebelling against everything I felt was being pressed on me. Religion, clothing, popular groups, etc. I felt like my life was crap, I was chronically depressed and I wanted to act out against everything. That is when I took it too far and set fire to those two port-a-johns. That was my first experience doing something really bad and illegal and honestly I liked it. It was different and I felt like it satisfied my urge to rebel. Then again when I got caught with it, I broke down and admitted to it quickly. As much as I felt good while doing it, it felt so terrible after. I decided to lay low for a while after that, but I never forgot that feeling of utter joy and excitement doing something bad. That feeling was what came up again in 9th grade. In the beginning of ninth grade, feeling a lot of the same things I had before in middle school (the loneliness and the depression.), but on a bigger scale because now I felt like I really didn't matter being in a bigger school. Home life was nothing desirable for me and I felt like I needed something else to make me whole. That was when, in photography class, I heard a couple upperclassmen talking about their drug experiences and how much fun they had while high. To me, at the time, that seemed like such a bad thing, considering how I have always been told drugs and smoking were such awful and evil things. Knowing that I had an urge to try it. I had some feeling deep inside that it would be cool and an awesome experience to get high. Like I said I didn't feel whole and I had a sense this could help. I went home immediately and researched every aspect of marijuana on a website called "www.Erowid.org". After a day or so I deemed Marijuana to not be nearly as bad as it is made out to be, by DARE and etc. so I decided to confront the upperclassmen in my photography class and ask him to get me some. He agreed for a price. I paid him and he delivered. I remember I had it all planned out and researched. I even went so far as to find out that new smokers don't often get high their first time, so I looked up proper techniques on how to smoke it properly. I remember feeling so nervous, scared and excited right before I decided to do it. I was alone in my room at about midnight, on my laptop. I had been burning incense about a week or two before I did it because I knew I would need to cover the smell and it would be better to get you two used to such activity before I did so. So I did it. I smoked the pot out of this little glass pinch-pipe the upperclassman gave me and it worked. In about five minutes I was so stoned I didn't know what was going on. I distinctly remember falling out of my chair and just laughing uncontrollably. I had never felt anything so amazing in my life and so awesome. It was like nothing could hurt me. Nothing was bad and I didn't have to care about anything. Everything was just good and happy. I am going to take a quick break from this to let you know that I was just talking with someone here and he said something that I want to include and let you know. The first time I used an illegal drug was not because of peer pressure. Peer pressure was not my cause for doing drugs because the first time I used I was completely alone... I was so depressed and so unhappy in my life that this is what I used to fill the void. This was what I used to cover the pain and make me feel whole. I never really understood my feelings at the time and I couldn't place it until now, but I never felt whole. I never felt loved and I never felt like I mattered. I couldn't deal with those feelings because I couldn't understand them so they just caused me torment and depression. I drowned that depression out with my new best friend: Marijuana. This was my first experience with it. I want to say that drinking has never been a big thing for me so I don't pay a whole lot of credit to it. I honestly have been drunk less then 12 times and I don't really like it. Marijuana was the big one for me. Using gave me that feeling of doing something bad and different in my life. Like I was a rebel and I was sneaky because no one knew that when I was high. It gave me such a good feeling inside and I loved it. Over the first year I used it fairly often, a few times a week. Once a day to every other day. I got a lot of my friends started on it. Sam and Karl... I started them using pot. Though they never loved it like I did... I think that is because they never had the feelings I did. They never had the hate and loathing for sober life. For dealing with one's emotions. I hated it because they were so dark and messed up. Pot made me feel "normal". During this time I felt like life couldn't be better. My relationships and life at home wasn't great but hey! Anytime I felt bad I could just self medicate and I did that often. I did alright and school and things seemed to be going pretty well. I started getting into harder and harder drugs too during this time. The next drug I tried was cough syrup, specifically "Robitussin Cough Gels" aka Destromenthoraphan Hbr. This I researched as well, as I did with all the drugs I did. I would find around the maximum amount could be taken before "bad things" would start happening. I based this off of other people's experiences posted on the same website, (Erowid). (I figured this to be how I would use drugs "safely" and more or less I would have to say it worked considering I am still alive. I would always check different experiences and reports on the different drugs and judge what would be "safe" amounts to ingest. I used my own body like a lab-rat with those conclusions...) Anyways, I did Robitusson a "fair few times", aka around 10-15 times. I don't know how many exactly, I lost count. I tried mushrooms next and enjoyed those very much. I first did them at Aaron Gramann's house and we spent the night walking around the neighborhood and rolling around in the grass in the early morning hours. On mushrooms, like any hallucinogen, I felt like the world as I knew it was completely different. Like I was living in a different place all together and a different world. I loved mushrooms and have done them a lot, (probably 20 or more times). I have also done Ecstacy a multitude of times. Ecstacy was an awesome drug for any situation. It was like, pop this one little pill and I knew no negative feelings for 8 hours. It was like magic. I looked at all these drugs like magic potions and secret cures for all sorts of negative feelings I experienced. I felt like a doctor carrying around a bag of drugs, knowing that anything bad I felt I could fix, immediately. It made me feel cool and powerful, as well as secure and happy to know I didn't have to feel bad anymore as long as I had drugs to do. As I said I have done Ecstacy a few times, like 10-15 times. Sometimes I would snort it, or take multiple pills of it at a time, or over a period of time. These things were all experimented with during my first year of using drugs... I regret all of this and feel terrible to be able to admit it now, but things did get worse... Over the next year my drug use advanced even more to include more hardcore drugs, including Cocaine, LSD, Mescaline, and all sorts of different drugs. In ad dition to doing these drugs I also used all the other ones more frequently and smoked pot constantly. By this time there had been some police encounters and a lot of stupid illegal activity in my life that only fueled my negative feelings. Those negative feelings then fueled my desire to do more drugs and the spiral just kept going. LSD aka Acid, was a lot like mushrooms but a lot cheaper, easier to hide and lasted more then twice as long. I used it a lot. I took it in school more then once and I am surprised I never got caught... I did cocaine a few times with my friends. They were always more interested in it then I was but I admit I enjoyed it a bit and bought it on a few different occasions. I have done Mescaline once and numerous amounts and kinds of different prescription pills. I used adderall in a bad way, aka used to get high on, probably a dozen or so, times, other then that I popped it at will to help concentrate in school. This is pretty much my drug history at least all the drugs I have done. I used to boast that I have done them all but crack and heroin. I have never done crack, or heroin, or opium, or PCP, or Ketamine. Those are the big ones I haven't, but I have done everything I have mentioned here. I have done crystal meth once and only once. I would never mess with that again. Not because it is awesome and I am afraid of being addicted to it or anything, but honestly I don't like it and it is expensive. Speaking of expenses I feel I should mention my money conditions through all of this. I manipulated constantly to get more money through you, Dad. Every dollar you gave me I used for one of a few different expenses. I bought drugs, I gambled, I bought gas and food. That was it. Anything else I ever asked money for was a lie over the past couple years. Honestly with the money you gave me and everything I wouldn't of been able to afford all of my drugs, so I had a job with a few of my friends. I was the driver and transporter of drugs. I used to make trips downtown every day to go with friends to the dealer's houses to buy all the different kinds of drugs. I got discounts for this and free drugs. I used to feel like such a big-shot being the only kid in my class with a car and a license. I also used that position for a lot of evil things. To go off on a tangent that I forgot to mention, my use of cigarettes. Honestly I would smoke 1/4-1/2 a pack of cigarettes a day at most, while sharing with friends. I never have smoked very many cigarettes and very rarely when I was not high already. That is pretty much all I have to say about that. I think this is pretty much everything about my drug use. I used a lot and mixed a lot of drug combinations together. I have a lot of really wild memories and some nights I can't really remember at all. The gist of all of it though is listed here, as best as I can name it. My drug use continued to worsen and worsen up until I came here to midwest academy. I feel like I must confess the only time in the past couple years that I have not been high was that month I was in rehab and within the hour of being home I was smoking pot again. Rehab was nothing more then expensive way for me to hang out for a month, smoke free cigarettes, and get "hook ups" for more drug contacts.

I am now going to talk about illegal activities. My illegal activities are very extensive and happened very frequently. People say insanity is doing the same thing over and over again and expecting different results, (especially with the police catching me with drugs). Well, I got caught 1/100 times I was doing something illegal. My friends and I smoked everyday, in parks, in houses or just driving around in various people's cars, or my own. We would do the stupidest things all the time. For instance stealing. I used to go with a couple people on stealing runs and just shop lift anything we could carry out of places. We would honestly drive around to different stores like Meijer or Kmart and steal all we could carry and leave. I have never been caught for shop lifting. We also stole alcohol and cigars from grocery stores and cigar shops. I used to sneak out every single night of the week and mess around with friends. We would do drugs, watch movies, gamble or other activities Car-hopping was a favorite game of mine. It consisted of walking around at night and trying to open car doors on the side of the streets. If the door opened you stole everything you could out of the car and ran off. More then once have I been chased by people for this. This is honestly one of the stupidest things I have ever done...But very profitable. I used to get a lot of money and expensive things out of cars. I would then sell those things to friends and buy drugs with the money. After I got caught for this that one time I never really did it again but before that I did it very often. As I said I snuck out every night to screw around. Sometimes I would be out until 5-6:00 AM, come home and then not go to school because I said I had insomnia. Truth is, I never tried to sleep at night. I was going all night long and most of the day. I skipped school an amazing amount of times as you both probably already know and am amazed myself I didn't get in more trouble sooner over that. I used to think I was so good at sneaking out. I would roll my car out of the garage on neutral and start it in the street and be off from there. I honestly used to get up, go to school, or skip with some people, be out all day until midnight, come home for 15 minutes while I made sure you were asleep, mom and then I would leave again and come back early in the morning. This was my routine for more nights then I can remember. I also was present and participated in a lot of different drug deals. Though I never dealt drugs myself, ever, I participated by driving dealers to locations or buyers to dealers. I also participated in buying more drugs from more people then I can remember, on many occasions. I have never obeyed curfew either. It has just been luck that I have never been caught for it more. I know I have been a few times but I honestly was out every night for the past year or so. Also concerning illegal activities, as you both know I tried to grow Marijuana in my closet and that didn't work, but that wasn't the only time. I grew pot with a friend in Burbank park and did so successfully. Successfully meaning we did in fact harvest it and consume it. I am having difficulty really remembering a lot more that has happened or I have done. Concerning illegal activities in my car, I never was really an unsafe driver at all. I obeyed all of the traffic laws and didn't speed. I know on a couple occasions I have said some pretty stupid dramatic things about how I was speeding going 100+ miles per hour and going to run my car off a bridge, but those were honestly lies. I have always been a safe driver, I feel. As you both know I have had a couple accidents with my car and a couple of which I feel were my fault. Despite this I still feel I am a good driver. I drove high literally everyday and I don't believe that hindered my driving ability in the least. Even so it is stupid, illegal and irresponsible as was a lot of my behaviors during this time. I think that is all I really need to say about that. I know I have stolen a lot and have done a lot of illegal activities concerning drugs. In conclusion that is all I really have to say concerning my illegal activities. A lot of drugs, a good amount of stealing and a lot of not obeying laws, in general.

Now concerning sex and women. I first want to start off by saying Mom, I have never felt like you really loved me. I have so many feelings that I have harbored inside that have hurt me for so long. I feel like you always made me feel stupid and worthless and above all else wrong. I was always wrong and you were always right and this created 1001 problems for me. I feel a lot of my problems and dark feelings that I was trying to drown out, were caused by this. Not that I have not contributed in my own ways and you haven't done your best, but this is just the way I feel. I never have felt like I have had that relationship of a loving female figure in my life. That is why I believe I am the way I am towards women. I respect them very much and feel like they are better then me a lot of the time. I feel that is brought on by you, mom always having to make me feel wrong and you always having to be right. I am also very insecure about myself and feel I need to have a girlfriend at all times. I need someone to love me because I have never really felt that from home. In addition to needing to feel loved I also am very "clingy" to girlfriends. I feel I need them. I need someone to love me constantly. I also know that as long as I have been old enough to date, or " of 8th grade... I had a certain relationship at the time that I had been in for a very long time. In fact I had a feeling from it that I was sure was love and everything was going so amazing concerning it. I looked to her for everything and was the main focus of my life but still all the time something was missing. Something still wasn't adding up inside of me and I wanted more. That is when I looked to sex, for that. I had sex with her in 8th grade. This is the first time I ever had sex and I am not going to go into any detail on with who or how many times, or what...But this is the only person I have ever had sex with. To be honest it wasn't near what people make it out to be and when it also didn't fill the void inside of me things fell apart and we ended up breaking up a few months later. This is WAY out of my comfort zone to talk about or admit, but it is the messed up truth. I especially want to indicate how sorry I feel for this event, like all of the events I have mentioned here in this letter. I regret all of these terrible events in my life so much and I want nothing more then to put them all behind me and just move on. I feel this is a first big step so everyone is on the same page. I have been avoiding really writing this all out in more detail for a long time. I know I wrote to you Dad, once a little while ago, about some of this but I feel I need to get this all out in a more depth and formal way and send it to both of you. Honestly my last attempt at writing a confession letter was like a brief summary of everything that I put together in an hour. I want to put much more effort into this work, which I am spending much more time on. Anyways, that is pretty much it with sex. Concerning women I have had a lot of relationships and a lot of failed ones. The one thing that has been consistent is my constant desire for another relationship and my clinginess to every girl that I am with. That is everything I feel I should say on that.

    I am now going to take a chance to just write and ramble about things that come to mind about my past and things I want to confess and get out there. This is a letter designed for me and you guys both to get on the same page and just so there is a common understanding of everything that has gone on. I regret so much that I have done and more then anything, I hold shame for it all, and a lot of it. I beat myself up constantly for what I have done and how much I regret the past. The past is my biggest enemy right now because it haunts me constantly. I really hope with this letter I will be able to get even some more peace with everyone and everything in my life. I just want to move on and make better decisions from here on out. I am so thankful for being able to come to this program and realize all of the things I have. I feel like genuinely I know what I was doing wrong at home and what I need to do in order to have a much more successful future. Since I have been here at Midwest Academy I have a knowledge now that I am going to have a future and it is going to be an awesome one. I know now my true potential and I feel I can do it. I can have a successful life. I have so many regrets in my life and so little successes. I never want to be where I am now again. I never want to be able to look back on only a life of ruin again. I am genuinely committed to changing these things and having a better life for the future. I want to talk about disrespect a little bit too. It honestly has never been a real concern with me. I mean, I have always felt like I was being screwed so I could treat you guys how I wanted. I know I have always gotten pretty much everything that I have wanted but there was always something missing. Something emotional that always ate at me. I blamed you guys for my problems and that justified every time that I was angry, or upset and said a bunch of crap that was terrible and I didn't mean. Sure I regretted it all and am so sorry for it all but I could always justify my behavior with the fact that in the end it was all your fault. I know now it wasn't and I played a part in everything. I know that everything has been my choice and my decisions. I take full accountability for it all and I am going to take full accountability for my very successful future too. I want to let you know that everything and anything I have said to you disrespectful and mean, or terrible, I am sorry for it. I am sorry for it all and I regret it all so much and I hope you will both just look to the future and judge me, based on how I am now and not the past. I also want to go into some detail on my relations with people from a fighting stand point. I know a lot of people here at midwest, have been in a lot of fights and some have even shot, stabbed, or killed a person. I want to let you both know I have never been in any sort of fight whatsoever. I have never shot a gun or anything like that. I have seen a lot of guns and played with some but never shot one, (including a Romanian AK-47 assault rifle). I hope that can put your mind at ease a bit. I was never one to act in violence. I really don't believe in it much. I have said a lot of stupid things to shock or frighten people but what I really mean believe I keep to myself. I enjoy getting reactions out of people and I often do things and say things to get certain reactions. I also want to mention that despite all I have said I still have no different opinion concerning drugs. I don't believe that drugs are any worse or better then when I arrived here and my opinion of myself concerning them is unwavering. I don't feel I have any addiction or anything of the sort. I honestly know I could never use again and be fine and content with it. My only concern is Marijuana. I had a lot of fun times with Marijuana but I don't know if I would be able to go back to it. I know I want to use it again, on a recreational basis, nothing like I did back home, but I am not sure what that would mean. I feel like I was using it for all the wrong reasons at home before and was using it and drugs in general as a crutch more then anything. I really don't know concerning the whole issue and that is going to be a decision to be made later. Anyways, I have been working on this little by little over the course of about a week and I really don't know what else to add. There are a lot of things I could say and I have said all that come to mind. I don't really know what else to put in here, but I know there is more you both still don't know. I think this is how it will always be because honestly, I can't name every time I did something bad, (there simply isn't a way to list it all). I hope you both understand this letter for what it is. It is my feeble attempt to get everything out there and understood. I am aware of all of the terrible things I have done and said. I have hurt a lot of people and myself most of all. I want you both to know that I love you and please understand, things how they were, as I described here, will never be again. You have my full assurance. Well that is it. I hope neither of you are angry or too upset. I love you both...

Love,
Ryan"

As scary as some of the revelations in this letter were to me, I also had to recognize that it was a huge step for my son. Not only did he "come clean" with, I would have to say, nearly all of his missteps, he also recognized that his actions were wrong and needed correction. Just to admit all of this and apologize for it was a big "cleansing" moment for him.

DAILY LIFE- A REAL "ROLLERCOASTER"

Ryan's stay at Midwest was, as with the rest of his life before and since a "rollercoaster". He had many ups and downs along the way, as are reflected in many of his other letters. Ryan was confronted, for the first time in his life, sorry to say, with the notion that he had to "earn" privileges and freedoms.

One of the basic requirements of this program is to progress through a series of "levels". At each level, more privileges are earned. For example, a student must be at level 3 to get to receive a phone call from home. This takes most kids anywhere from 3 to 5 months of following the rules and earning points. Just think of this. In order to even get to talk to your parents over the phone, you have to wait patiently, and follow the rules for 3 to 5 months! Then you must be a level 4 in order to get to visit a parent. In our case, this took about 7 months. The kids also have to attend and pass the seminars referred to above as part of the "rite of passage" to earn these privileges.

Obviously, as the earlier material shows, Ryan did not have a background or experience following rules, earning privileges and the like. This whole concept was new to him, and he struggled with it mightily. He had several incidents of going on probation, losing his points and dropping a level, and being denied privileges already earned. Despite this, he continued to make progress overall and, while sometimes taking one step forward and 2 steps back, continued to get better.

At the same time, his emotional and anxiety issues were always in the forefront. Like his mother, he is a very emotional kid and has difficulty controlling this aspect on life. I arranged for him to see a psychologist while in Iowa, and he was prescribed Depakote, a strong psycotropic medication that is normally prescribed for people with bipolar disorder. The Psychologist called it a "mood stabilizer", and Ryan seemed to me to be calmer while on these meds. (He, of course, denied that they did anything at all for him).

What Ryan's psychologist explained to us was that, while Ryan "gets upset about the same types of things most people do, his reactions are much stronger and they stay with him longer" than they do for most people. He felt this condition was partly environmental (learned) and part heredity. In any event, he told Ryan this "intense emotionality" was something he would struggle with probably for life.

Character Building vs. Complete High School

One issue that developed was whether Ryan would get to come home when he turned 18 in September of 2006, or if I would set a requirement that he graduate the "character building" program, which the school recommended they complete. I had told Ryan that when he finished high school he could come home.

CHAPTER 11
COMING HOME SEPTEMBER, 2006

On Ryan's 18th birthday, September 27, 2006, I made the long drive to Iowa to pick up my son who I hoped and prayed had changed. He swore he had. Over the last couple months he had completed high school and earned a diploma. He also assured me he was very confident in his ability to come home, get a job and start going to college. He was determined and confident his life would now be "back on track".

He moved in with me to the condo I bought the year before after I had moved out. The first couple weeks were ok, but I was soon disappointed when he announced that he didn't feel he should start college right away. Because he had been gone so long and had been in such an intense environment, he wanted to "take some time off". He said he would get a job and save some money and go back to school in winter quarter in January, 2007. I did not insist on his starting school, and it seemed I had to be constantly on him about finding a job.

He did get hired part time making sandwiches at a Subway restaurant, but soon I was starting to see some old patterns creep back into his life and to our interactions. He started staying out late, sometimes until 5 or 6 am the next morning, and sleeping most of the day until well into the afternoon. He stopped taking the Dapakote medication because he claimed it made him feel "dead inside" with no emotions. (I honestly think he was experiencing for the first time what it might have felt like to have more normal emotionality and it felt foreign to him!) My relationship with Ryan began deteriorating about this time. I was complaining about his lifestyle, and he got tired of my interfering in his "freedom".

He started to complain about having to live with me, and said he wanted to get a roommate around his own age, who could share expenses. "Nobody my age lives with their dad. I can't have friends over (particularly girls, and that's why I'm gone all the time", he would say. He thought I should move in with my new friend Karen, whom I had met at work and fell in love with. We were now engaged and spending most of our time together anyway. I spoke to Ryan's psychologist about this and he agreed with Ryan. He said now that he's an adult, you have to let him be accountable for his own actions and "you can't police him every day-it will drive you crazy!" I guess this was what I wanted to hear, and I was having trouble getting along with Ryan. I didn't like his lifestyle, and his emotions and our interactions were getting increasingly difficult to bear, again.

Ryan found a friend with a full-time job who agreed to pay some rent, and I thought this might be a good influence on him. I jumped at the chance to leave!

CHAPTER 12

HEROIN!

Before long, in early 2007, we had to basically evict Ryan's friend from my condo. He did not pay his (very small) rent timely. He was an alcoholic and, between the 2 of them, they had "trashed" the place. Ryan was working but spending all his money "somehow". He was not paying me rent and had begun begging me for money again. I, who had not learned anything from my own experiences before, once again gave in and started "enabling" him. The police had been called multiple times with complaints of loud partying and I received a phone call from a neighbor who worked at the Dublin police Department that the condo was being watched by some detectives as an establishment where drug deals were being made!

After we asked his friend to leave, Ryan found a girlfriend to move in and this sounded to me like a stabilizing influence on him. The girl seemed to have her head on straight, and seemed more mature than he was. At least it seemed that way to me at the time (or maybe it's what I wanted to believe.)

{I will digress for a moment here and say that this began a period that lasted several years of my paying all Ryan's (and the girlfriend's) living expenses. Both of them were living rent free on me in 3 different apartments. I paid all the utilities and other bills, too.}

Back to 2007. The Sunday before Easter I received a call from Ryan who was desperate to talk with me and told me he needed my help and wanted me to come over right away. When I arrived he said, "I don't know how to tell you this, but for the last "several weeks" I have been experimenting with heroin. It had gotten out of control, he thought he was addicted and needed help.

Dad sprung into action again, making phone calls and checking with my insurance to see if I could arrange treatment for him. On Monday morning (I was always a very efficient "fixer"), I arranged for him to check into the Woods at Parkside, a drug and alcohol treatment facility in town. We arrived that morning and Ryan was given an assessment by an experienced counselor, a man in his 50s who was a recovering heroin addict. The man asked him what I now believe to be the most pertinent question I had heard. It was "how many friends do you have, that you can share anything with about your life, who are not drug users or addicts?" Astonishingly, Ryan could not come up with a single one!

The man replied, "We can get you off heroin, that's easy. It will take about 4 days, and you will be sick, but we will treat you for the worst of that. The question is, what is your plan to stay clean? When all your friends are drug addicts or abusers, you have a very slim chance of staying sober". Ryan thought this concept to be ridiculous and said so to me and the counselor.

Anyway, he stayed there for about 5 days, felt better and declared himself basically "cured". I took him to my mother's house that weekend for Easter, but was awakened in the middle of the night with Ryan having gut-wrenching sickness. I rushed him to the Emergency Room of a Dayton, Ohio hospital. It seemed he was still experiencing withdrawal symptoms from the heroin!

CHAPTER 13

ENABLING AND MORE INSANITY

Over the next couple years, many things happened. As mentioned previously when talking about Ryan's high school years, my memory of events and their sequence is rather blurry to me at this time. All I know for sure is that I lived in a fog where the world seemed to be passing me by. The circumstances were beyond insanity. Looking back, I felt at the time these issues were all Ryan's fault. Now, with the enlightenment of Nar-Anon, I clearly recognize my own fault and contribution to these events.

With my total assistance, financially and otherwise, Ryan lived in 4 separate apartments where I paid <u>all</u> the rent, utilities, moving costs and all other living expenses. In most of these places, he had a girlfriend living with him at my expense. Between apartments, rehabs and jail, I paid $60 per month to store his property!

In addition to all the above, I paid for the gas, maintenance and insurance on his car for several years. Other car expenses included:

- repair following several accidents (costing at least twice the initial purchase price)
- tires when they wore out (or, damaged from driving impaired)
- brake jobs
- towing and impoundment fees

On top of all these expenditures, Ryan was frequently able to manipulate hundreds of dollars cash from me, often on a weekly basis. I am absolutely sure at this point that I covered his drug costs. I was, to use an analogy I thought up recently, figuratively supplying him with guns and bullets to play Russian Roulette with his life. The stories he came up with to get this money were nothing short of ingenious, and could be the topic of a book all their own. I wanted to believe him so bad!

Ryan got into trouble, as mentioned previously, with the law on many occasions, and additional expenditures I made were for:

- 3 different lawyers to represent him
- bail to get him out of jail
- fines paid off

I was called by the police to come and get him out of jail in the middle of the night more times than I can remember!

<u>Rehabs and Confinement</u> Ryan definitely was on the "rehab tour", as I heard a Nar-Anon friend describe it, spending time in 11 different residential treatment and confinement facilities, as follows:

1. 30 days Hazelden, MN (my cost, $9,000)
2. 11 months, Midwest Academy (my cost, $50,000)
3. 2 weeks (on different occasions) Ohio state University Hospitals.
4. 1 week, Woods at Parkside, Columbus (my cost, $1,000)
5. 30 days, Maryhaven. Columbus, OH (no cost)
6. 2 days Salvation Army drug program (no cost, but Ryan was ejected for going through heroin withdrawal)
7. 30 days, Franklin County Jail (2 stints, no cost)
8. 90 days, CTC, Lancaster, Oh (no cost)
9. 33 days, Richland County Jail, Mansfield, OH (no cost)
10. 2 weeks, Glenbeigh, Cleveland, OH (no cost)
11. 200+ days (2 admissions) Quest Wilson Hall, Massillon, OH (no cost)

As you can see above, I finally stopped paying for this stuff. But, the other noteworthy thing to see is that the confinements got longer and more serious over time!

CHAPTER 14

STORM CLOUDS OVER A NEW MARRIAGE

As discussed before, I got re-married on June 30, 2007 to a wonderful woman named Karen. She is totally different than my first wife, in many ways. She is stable emotionally and very mature despite being 9 years younger than I. Her presence in my life has made a total difference in the way I view the world, life in general, and the problems my son was having.

Despite all of her love and understanding, she immediately found herself on the emotional rollercoaster with me, involving all the insanity that goes along with having an addicted loved one. I soon found myself on the verge of another marital breakup.

I am definitely not proud of the role I played in the events described in the previous chapter. Maybe, just maybe, had I read a book like this one earlier in my life, things might have turned out differently. At least I keep thinking this, and it's one reason I decided to write about my experiences. I second guess myself all the time. I realize now that doing all the things I did probably enabled Ryan to continue living the life he was living, perhaps for several years longer than if I had put a stop to it sooner. All of this he did at grave risk to his life. Karen, it turned out, in witnessing all this, was able to see the insanity and risk this represented.

They say one addict or alcoholic impacts the lives of 5 or 6 other people besides himself. In my case, my wife Karen, whom I love dearly, was severely impacted. Having to witness and live through this dysfunction she saw in front of her. Karen, I am deeply sorry.

Almost from the very beginning of my relationship with Karen, in 2005, my behavior as it concerned Ryan, seriously affected our relationship and nearly destroyed it before it had a chance to get off the ground. The reason I emphasize my behavior, is that I now refuse to make myself the victim of my son's poor choices. I also had free will and free choice.

Karen knew intuitively that the things I was doing with Ryan were wrong and she didn't know the half of it! She saw a person she loved being jerked, pulled and manipulated by an addict. She saw me jump when he called and heard me being victimized by verbal abuse and threats whenever he did not immediately get what he wanted. This was usually money, but often rides to visit his dealers and drug using "friends". She saw me take the telephone to the bedroom so I could be "on call" for him around the clock, and to be prepared to face my worst fears: a phone call in the middle of the night to say "come pick him up at jail", or the hospital calling telling me he was dead of an overdose.

Karen then would see me leave in the middle of the night to help him, bail him out, pick him up at the jail or hospital. She saw me leave to go see him when he wanted something (money), and her questioning of me and my own behavior became so uncomfortable, I began lying just like the addict. (When you find yourself doing this, remember you are just as sick as the addict!)

These things made her feel sorry for me at first, but they eventually lead to her verbally objecting to my behavior. She knew intuitively that none of this was helping Ryan, and it constituted abuse of me! Finally, she rightly began to lose respect for me. Ryan and I had lost respect for me as well. I just didn't realize it yet.

There were many arguments and tension between us at a time when, as newlyweds, we could and should have been having some of our closest times together as a new couple. Talk about the honeymoon being over. This behavior brought it to a screeching halt! Obviously none of this was fair to her or our brand new marriage. Only her patience, love and understanding saved it, and I'm frankly surprised we survived it!

How did I cope with this level of stress on our new relationship? I lied and concealed my own behavior and participation in Ryan's insanity! I began acting just like an addict myself: lying and manipulating. Karen did not know the size or the extent of my financial participation in this situation. I made up reasons to maintain separate bank accounts (I don't want to get into a situation like in my first marriage where my wife spent more money than I thought we could afford without my consent). This kept her from seeing the records of just how much money was going out the door to support his lifestyle choices and kept me from having the discomfort of trying to defend it. I literally had no backbone where dealing with either of them was concerned!

I did all this, I have since figured out, to avoid confrontations with either Karen or Ryan. As I later learned in Nar-Anon, it's not uncommon that the disease of the co-dependent parent is just as serious, warped and irrational as that of the addict himself! This disease of addiction quickly swept its way through my new family the way it had in the first one, only worse. Only God and Karen's love for me could have saved our marriage.

I feel the need to once again stress that this was not Ryan's fault. His choices were certainly deplorable, but nobody held a gun to my head and forced me to do the things I did to participate in this insanity. I know now that my behavior is the only behavior I have any control over. Nobody could have forced me to do the things I did without my consent.

Karen, I am so very sorry! You waited a long time in your life single, because you wanted to make sure that if you got married, it was the right situation. You certainly experienced more than your share of bad relationships before I came along. I deeply regret putting you through this. You are a wonderful human being, whom I love very dearly. I really admire your ability to forgive and "bounce back". You do it consistently and I love you very, very much! I hope you can find it in your heart to totally forgive me for all of this. (I think you will or already have).

CHAPTER 15

THE CASH STOPS (FOR NOW)

New Years Eve, 2009. Ryan called to ask for his normal "couple hundred bucks". I said no. I then went on to outline for him the new approach we had decided upon implementing. It went something like this. For the time being, I agreed to pay half his rent, plus supply a food card for the grocery store ($80 per week) and a gasoline card ($30 per week). As anticipated, the arguing immediately started.

"Why is this happening now", and "How can you just change like this without advanced notice". I made clear that I was not debating the matter, and that, in addition, I would no longer be "on call", answering his phone calls anytime he wished to speak with me. (Previously he would call sometimes multiple times per day, and tie me up for an hour or more at a time)

To escape the arguing, I finally put the phone on silent mode, and left it in my office instead of carrying it constantly and leaving it beside the bed at night, just waiting for the next "crisis" call. This was one of several "firsts" for me in beginning (just beginning as it turned out) to take back my life.

Ryan's response? 10 to 15 voice mails over the next 24 hours, and a like number of text messages trying to get me to talk to him, and using all of his best manipulative techniques. "You're a bad father", "you've never been there for me", "you abandoned my mother, now you're abandoning me", "you care more about your new happy, little family than you do me".

While I listened to and read the messages, I did not respond for the first couple days. This was difficult for me, as Ryan had learned to "jerk my chain" and always get some kind of response, over a 7 year period since he was 14! After about a day and a half, the messages finally subsided and eventually stopped for a couple days.

CHAPTER 16

APRIL, 2010- ANOTHER DUI

I was lying in bed awake trying to sleep and worrying as I usually did, when my phone rang about 12:30am. "Dad", Ryan slurred, "I really screwed up. I wrecked my car and the damned police are charging me with DUI". I asked if he was hurt, and he answered "no". He asked if I would come and pick him up at a downtown hospital. I hemmed and hawed mentally, knowing he needed to experience the consequences of his bad choices, but finally agreed to come and pick him up.

Because the hospital had essentially kicked him out, he was sitting on a bench in front of the emergency room entrance. Had I been much longer, they would have chased him off or had him arrested because of the shape he was in. The first thing I noticed when I arrived was that he was visibly, totally messed up on something! He apologized, then immediately curled up on the front seat and went to sleep as I drove him to his apartment that I was paying half the expenses on, his girlfriend the other half.

When we arrived, I had to help him to the door and put his key into the lock for him. He was so wobbly he could not walk without assistance, and I could barely understand his speech. Despite this he claimed to have fallen asleep at the wheel when driving, due to insomnia and problems with anxiety that kept him up. He claimed to have only taken the prescribed dose of his anxiety medication, Xanax.

I told Ryan to call me the next day, I got home about 2:30 or 3:00 am. How many times would I let this happen before I learned my lesson? How many times before he learned his? I had lost track of the number of times I had been called, in the dead of night, and dutifully (like the "loving father" I had convinced myself I was) drove off to yet another police station or hospital to make sure my son got home safely.

Over the next 24 hours, I learned that the car was impounded, had been totally demolished, and Ryan was lucky to be alive and that he had not killed anyone else! Later on, as learned more and more "facts" (they always came out over time when he was sober and in a mood to come clean). He admitted he was prescribed 2 pills per day, to be taken 12 hours apart, but had taken 2 at once. I also later learned from his girlfriend, that he had often taken Xanax with heroin to enhance the "high". Anyway, the car I had been dumb enough to buy him when he turned 16 in 2004 was finally gone, and nobody was hurt or killed. At my Nar-Anon parent group meeting that week, I proclaimed how grateful I was that no one was injured or killed and that, just as wonderfully, his driving days were over for the time being, hopefully a long time!

When Ryan went to court on the new charges, he filled out paper work to try to secure legal representation from the Public Defender. This was not his first choice, but I had told him after paying for an attorney to get him "off the hook" on 12 out of 13 juvenile charges, that I would never pay for an attorney for him again (a promise I finally kept). However, because I had supported him and declared him as a dependent on my tax return, he was ineligible for public defender assistance. So, reluctantly, I agreed to talk to the prosecutor and Judge and see what I could do to assist him. (I was committed to help him only to get treatment if available).

Ryan entered a "not guilty" plea, and then we were able to get him accepted into the Franklin County Municipal Court Drug Court program, which is designed to help addicts get better while punishing them for their crimes. Acceptance into the program requires a guilty plea to the DUI, and mandatory weekly appearances in Drug Court, the possibility to weekly drug tests, and 3 years' probation.

CHAPTER 17

NAR-ANON AND AL-ANON

One of the very most important "life saving" decisions I made in early 2010 was to finally try Nar-Anon and Al-Anon meetings. Why this idea had not taken hold sooner is somewhat a mystery. I think the main reason most of the people in my situation are reluctant to attend meetings is the thought that "we" collectively (the people who are neither alcoholics nor drug addicts, but have them in our families) are not the ones with "the problem".

Al-Anon and Nar-Anon are both based upon the 12 steps of Alcoholics Anonymous, but are designed to help families (parents, siblings, spouses and others) who have an addict in their lives or families. However, when I attended any Al-Anon or Nar-Anon meeting, I was struck by the relatively small number of people in attendance. This is particularly true when contrasted against some of the large numbers of meeting and addicts in attendance at AA and NA. It has been reported that each addict adversely affects the lives of at least 5 other people in their family. Based upon this, you might think there could be as many as 5 times the number of family and friends of addicts seeking help from Nar-Anon or Al-Anon. That this is not even close to being the case suggests there are many, many more family members of addicts suffering from this disease than there are people seeking and receiving the wonderful help available!

Those of us attending these meetings are truly numbered among the "blessed" who are receiving help and support and have a chance to recover from a debilitating and disabling disease that is as real to us as that faced by the addict. It is my belief (and I've heard it expressed by countless others in these programs), that family members of addicts are often as sick, if not more sick, than the addict in the family. Why do I say it is "life saving"? There are many of us who see our own illness, as a family member of an addict, to be life-destroying for us and the addict. (Read on to learn more).

As of this writing, I have been attending these meetings more or less frequently over the course of about three years. In that amount of time, my own personal life has improved and I have grown tremendously! Am I cured? No, and I probably will never be "cured" of this illness. But, my life is improving and seems to get better exponentially by each step I take in the direction of lovingly "detaching" from my addicted son's life and outcomes. This is a difficult thing to do, but it is essential to having any hope of a successful life myself! Some of the people I know attending these meetings have been doing so for 5, 10, or 20 years or more! It is really quite remarkable. The longer they have been involved in this process (and it's definitely a "process" not a destination), the healthier they are.

One of the most startling announcements I heard in one of these meetings was made by the leader of the group I have been attending. He has been in attendance for the better part of 20 years. He declared that "I am grateful to the addicts (he has 3) in my life". I thought, how can he possibly be grateful for having this albatross of addiction around his neck that I have been suffering with for the better part of 10 years? He said it was because without the addicts in his life, he would never have attended these meetings. And, the meetings have, quite simply, changed his life!

He went on to explain that until he started attending these meetings (that a court ordered him to attend the first time), he thought of himself as "a God". He was a father with all the answers. He thought he was in control and knew what was best for others. All they (his kids) had to do was what he told them and all their problems would be solved.

What I have heard this man say many times over the several years was that he came to the meetings to try to figure out how to help his addicted daughters solve their problems, to help them stop using. What he learned and is grateful for, was that he "was a huge part of the problem". This lesson helped him not only to improve his life with his addicts, but with most other aspects of his life as well. I, too, have discovered the life-changing lessons these meetings have to offer. I am still learning, but I have discovered I can only help me, and that I and I alone am responsible for me, my own life, and happiness.

Most people who decide to attend Al-Anon or Nar-Anon meetings do so, at least initially, to figure out how to make their addict stop using or how to deal with them. What they soon discover is that these programs are really about them, not their addicts at all. It is about how we, as family members of addicts can learn to live a happier, healthier existence regardless of the choices our addicted family member makes. We also learn how powerless we really are over the disease of addiction and how to "detach with love" from our addicts and begin, at long last, to live happy lives ourselves.

Our programs are based upon the *12 Steps of Alcoholics Anonymous*, which are as follows:

1. We admitted we were powerless over alcohol addiction—that our lives had become unmanageable.
2. Came to believe that a Power greater than ourselves could restore us to sanity.
3. Made a decision to turn our will and our lives over to the care of God *as we understood Him.*
4. Made a searching and fearless moral inventory of ourselves.
5. Admitted to God, to ourselves, and to another human being the exact nature of our wrongs.
6. Were entirely ready to have God remove all these defects of character.
7. Humbly asked Him to remove our shortcomings.
8. Made a list of all persons we had harmed, and became willing to make amends to them all.

9. Made direct amends to such people wherever possible, except when to do so would injure them or others.
10. Continued to take personal inventory and when we were wrong promptly admitted it.
11. Sought through prayer and meditation to improve our conscious contact with God, *as we understood Him*, praying only for knowledge of His will for us and the power to carry that out.
12. Having had a spiritual awakening as the result of these Steps, we tried to carry this message to others, and to practice these principles in all our affairs.

I personally believe that the most immediately impactful of these steps is the first one, where we admit our powerlessness over addiction and the choices made by our addicted family member. It is also the step that may be the most difficult to accept. This is hard. As parents most of us believe not only that we are responsible for our children, but that we are in control of many aspects of their lives. I personally always felt responsible for Ryan, and labored under the delusion for many years, that I could help make him better. Certainly there were words I could say as a parent, or actions I could take to either change his behavior or get him to see the light of what he was doing to himself and his family.

The very first thing I learned about addiction in my very first Nar-Anon meeting was what the leader referred to as the 3 Cs:

1. You didn't cause it
2. You can't control it
3. You can't cure it

Wow, what a difficult thing this was to accept, but liberating at the same time! All three of these statements seemed counter intuitive to me as a parent. I had always believed that at least part of the addiction my son had was related to my poor parenting skills, lack of discipline or something! Ryan had even told me this in many conversations where he blamed me, his mother, his circumstances (you name it, anything but his own choices) for the predicament he was in.

I also had come to believe that I was responsible, accountable and possessed the means to get him to stop if only I said the right words, took the right actions, set the right rules, stopped enabling or any number of other actions. If only I could figure this thing out, Ryan could be convinced to stop using and begin living a productive life.

What I learned in reading the 1939 book *Alcoholics Anonymous*, (also referred to as "the Big Book"), is that alcoholics, and other addicts have a reaction to the substance that they describe as similar to an "allergy", that others don't have, which renders them unable to stop once they start taking the substance. The illnesses of alcoholism, and in my son's case heroin addiction, are both physically addictive, meaning that the person goes through serious physical withdrawal when the substance is removed from their daily lives.

This explains the baffling phenomenon where the addict seems to have no sense of caring about what they are doing to themselves. They literally will administer the substance to themselves with no regard to consequences. It steals all reason from them because they are ingesting it in order to avoid feeling sick. (In the heroin addict's case, they get what feels like deathly sick if they go for more than 12 hours without their "fix"!) I heard of one heroin addict who was an attorney, and said he lost his job, his license to practice, his home and his children. When he was in the throes of his addiction, he said, he would even have "sold his children for the next fix". There is no reasoning with this illness!

This realization of powerlessness can be enormously liberating for those of us who have spent years blaming ourselves, beating ourselves up, and struggling mightily to control, cure or persuade our addicts to stop killing themselves. (I say killing themselves because when my son heard the news that a well-known acquaintance died of an overdose of very pure heroin that was bought from the same dealer my son uses, this did not stop him. He literally played "Russian Roulette" with his life twice per day for a few years! And, I paid for the gun and bullets and put it in his hands (figuratively speaking, of course).

One of the most important things I learned was that it was not only possible, but necessary, to detach with love from your addicted child. It is possible to stop trying to control them and fix them. It is possible to stop punishing yourself and them. It is possible to love them and improve our relationships with them, and to set boundaries for them and ourselves that preserve our own peace and self-respect. We can resolve to protect our own homes and rights to a happy life and stop permitting another very ill individual the power to dictate our happiness.

Axioms

By attending meetings for Al-Anon and Nar-Anon, I have learned many truths or axioms ("nuggets of wisdom") I have heard that are priceless and deserve to be shared. Just a few are as follows:

1. How do you know when an addict is lying? His lips are moving!
2. Expectations are just premeditated resentments! (How many times have you made plans or had other expectations of your addict that were dashed when the addict either didn't show up, or was too "dope sick" to function?)
3. Addicts "lie, cheat and steal", so protect yourself!
4. What others think of me is none of my business! (I have heard so many people say they stopped sharing stories about their addicts with family or others who just don't understand, or blame you for what happened or have some really simple advice to follow that will solve the problem, e.g "just use tough love"!)
5. The pain I have experienced in my life has made me who I am today. Who am I to prevent my son from his "god given" right to experience pain? (Most of us as parents of addicts have tried to shield our children from the pain of the consequences of their bad choices).
6. Every addict I've met who recovered said "I didn't recover until …(fill in the blank):

    a. I lost my job
    b. I lost my kids or spouse
    c. I lost my home and had to live in a shelter
    d. I got sent to jail
    e. I overdosed and nearly died

    f. I got into a horrible accident
    g. I woke up lying in a pile of vomit on a crack house floor! (my personal favorite!)

If I try to step in and shelter my addicted love one from the pain of their choices, I am not only enabling them to continue risking his or her life, but I am very likely standing in the way of that one difficult experience that may trigger a recovery!

7. To recover an addict must change the people, places and things in their lives!
8. When the student is ready the teacher will appear! (This one I feel is really wise, because it underscores another important thing we learn, which is that nothing we can do will precipitate a recovery. The addict has to be ready himself! Then, once ready, they will do it on their own, not because of something we did).
9. If only the people in my life would play the roles I wrote for them in the "play of life" I meticulously wrote for them, everything would be fine. What I discovered was that they each wrote their own play!
10. It took me a long time attending these meetings to get to a point where I embraced and rejoiced when my addict experienced a painful consequence from his choices. This was because I know that from such experiences may come recovery!

These are all very hard lessons to learn, accept and implement in our lives. But, after hearing bits and pieces of this wisdom over and over (sometimes over many moths and years, it starts to sink in. When this happens we can slowly, little by little, begin to acquire the strength and liberation we need to start living our own lives! This wisdom is a great help in learning to stop participating in the daily insanity that swirls around the daily lives of these addicts. We then can stop being victims of our addicts' choices, stop contributing (with our time, attention and resources) to this insanity and choose a happy life for ourselves!

At this point in my own personal "recovery" (and it's every bit as much of a recovery for me as it is for my addict, the biggest "takeaway" I have from the meetings really stems form the *Serenity Prayer* we have all heard:

> "God, grant me the serenity to accept the things I cannot change, the courage to accept the things I can and the wisdom to know the difference"

Here is my personal interpretation of these words. It applies and has been helpful to me in my own life in many ways, not only in how I have chosen to react (or not react) to my son's illness, but in many other areas of life as well:

> I can only control my own thoughts, actions and reactions, not those of others. There are things that happen in life and people over which I have no control. If I continue to struggle to control those things over which I have no control, I can destroy my own life and well being in the process.

CHAPTER 18

JANUARY 14, 2011 FREE AT LAST?

Ryan ended up, after the accident and DUI conviction, spending 16 days in the county jail. After this, he was ordered sent to a facility in Lancaster, Ohio called CTC, which was a transitional facility, we later learned, mostly for felons returning from an Ohio prison who are being "transitioned" back into society. The Drug Court staff at the time described it as a "treatment facility". We later found out this was a total misnomer.

During Ryan's nearly 2 months at CT, I went to visit him, gave him some limited amounts of money to buy cigarettes and soda. I later found out he was buying drugs, and that drugs and their use were "rampant" at CTC. The drug court eventually stopped sending their participants there.

The drug court finally decided to release Ryan back into society after all this. Though the drug and alcohol counselors and the Judge were skeptical, Ryan's protestations that he had "hit rock bottom" from the experience of being in jail for the first time and CTC were ultimately persuasive. A key part of their willingness to give Ryan another chance at freedom centered on his having a place to live (an apartment his mother and I had agreed to provide some living assistance with, to include grocery cards, bus passes, etc.) On top of this, he had his Christmas gift of $1,500 from his grandmother (my mother) to "help him get on his feet". Once again, the desire to believe Ryan was on the way to recovery persuaded us to help him yet again!

We say all the time, and hear the families of other addicts say repeatedly, "what will it take for the addict to get the message and change his behavior"? I believe a more pertinent question for us to ask (as we can only control our own actions, might be "what will it take for me to get the message and change my behavior that is contributing to the situation?"

On the very day Ryan was released from confinement, he proceeded directly to an urgent care facility complaining of pain from a broken rib he told me he received at CTC when another inmate punched him for being a snitch. The urgent care doctor prescribed Vicodin, an opiate narcotic. Ryan was covered under my health insurance at work under a requirement of the new "Obamacare" law that mandated the offering of coverage to children of employees until age 26, regardless of whether they are full time students as had been the requirement before this law passed. When I later checked my insurance records, I learned he had filled 14 different prescriptions over the next 30 days.

Ryan told me he had consulted with one of the drug court's drug and alcohol counselors about the Vicodin. He cleverly told them it was a valid prescription for the intense pain he was having, but innocently asked them if they thought he should actually take it because of the risk of relapse! The counselors told him no, he should not take it because it was an opiate, but that if he really had pain he could try Tramadol, a nonopiate, less addictive painkiller. Ryan assured him he would switch the medications and bring both prescriptions into court so they could see them and to show that he had already taken some of the Vicodin (though less than was prescribed), thereby, in his mind, demonstrating that he was not "abusing" this opiate!

Over the next 30 days or so, Ryan seemed to be doing ok. He did, however, seem to be procrastinating on his job search and was traveling daily to visit a friend whom Ryan described as "clean" and they were "attending AA meetings together". About this time he also started asking for frequent rides to see this friend, and indicated he was running out of money and asking me to take him grocery shopping.

About 2 ½ to 3 weeks into his "freedom" he called me one day when I was on a business trip to Michigan, claiming to have a serious dilemma. One of his drug court probation requirements was that he was to call a particular phone number daily to inquire if he was scheduled for a random drug test that day. He found out he was scheduled that day and needed to report to the testing center between 1 and 4 pm for the test. His dilemma was that he could not be at 2 places at the same time. This happened to be, he said, the exact same time and date he was scheduled to be at his Intensive Outpatient program at Maryhaven.

He said he was likely to be drug tested there and didn't I think that would be acceptable. (He always seems to want me to agree with his planned course of action. I think that even though he was 22, if he could convince me, it would be acceptable. Or, maybe he planned to tell them I "advised" him to do it this way!) His stated concern was that because he could not get a ride to Maryhaven and the bus trip out there was very long, he would be unable to do both. He called the drug court and told them of his problem, and that he was planning to go to the Maryhaven appointment, where he would be tested and he could have the results sent to the court.

Later the same day, he called me again, told me he missed the bus to Maryhaven and the schedule was "screwed up". He said he would have to reschedule his appointment. In the meantime, he had also missed the teasing window at the court, arriving 5 minutes late. So, no drug test that day! It seemed curious to me that the entire set of circumstances resulted in no drug test either place. I asked him if this could be a problem for him, and he said he didn't think so, as he had made a legitimate attempt and had a good explanation.

CHAPTER 19

(2/18-3/14) BACK TO JAIL!

I called Ryan the morning of Friday February 18 and offered to give him a ride to his weekly drug court appearance, that he was obligated to make every Friday at 11. He was prepared to take the bus, but he said yes, I could take him. He also asked if I could come back and pick him up afterwards and give him a ride to Aaron's house. I had other duties and told him no, he would need to take the bus there.

Several hours after dropping him off at the court, I received a call from my emotionally distraught son. "Dad, I hate to tell you, I screwed up again!. I'm back in the Jackson Pike jail. I flunked a drug test for heroin and they caught me. It's my fault, my choice and I have to live with it. I'm sorry!".

He proceeded to spill the beans on what he had done. When he went to the urgent care facility (first day out of jail) he manipulated to get an opiate, Vicodin. He had concocted a "story" for this, and appeared to be honest in telling the court counselors about it, at the same time being careful to tell them he had already taken a small amount of the Vicodin but assuring them he would switch to Tramadol out of concern for his opiate addiction. Ryan believed this "legitimate" prescription for an opiate would provide a "cover story" if he failed another drug test for opiates.

What he hadn't counted on was the greater sophistication of the modern drug tests, which cannot only distinguish the exact opiate being used, but the amounts. He said "I met a guy at CTC who told me he had covered his heroin use for 3 months by taking the same prescription bottle to court week after week!"

At this point I really began to realize that I was learning something from my year in the Nar-Anon parent meetings. I was not surprised, maybe a little disappointed, but had a reaction I did not expect. I thought (but did not say) "Good, he's receiving a serious consequence for his bad choice. Maybe it's a trigger for a recovery at long last, who knows. He's safe and can't take drugs while he's there".

This reaction surprised me. For 22 years I had always tried to rescue him and shield him from any pain. What right did I have to shield him from pain he could learn from. Hadn't I experienced pain in my life and learned valuable lessons that made me change my behavior? What was it about me that made me feel so uncomfortable with the notion of Ryan experiencing the pain resulting from his bad choices? Was I contributing to this addiction?

Over the next three weeks I received, almost daily, a collect call from Ryan at the jail. In nearly all of these calls was the anguish of not knowing how long he would be there. Ryan had never been good at uncertainty. He did not have the patience for it and had always tried to exercise control over his circumstances, and anyone who tried to control them (and him) became the enemy! "What was the next step and when?", "Why can't the drug court and public defender get me out of here sooner, or at least tell me where I'm going next (and when)?"

One of the calls dealt with the anguish of receiving a summons to appear back in the Upper Arlington Mayor's Court for a probation revocation hearing. This is the court where Ryan was first charged with DUI in July, 2008. One of the conditions of that probation was that he not drink alcohol, use drugs, drive under the influence, or receive other charges for similar offenses.

The magistrate in that court had a reputation for being tough on repeat offenders and Ryan still had 177 days of jail time "on the shelf", (meaning suspended time during probation and good behavior that could be re-imposed for a violation.) Under Ohio law the judge is empowered to sentence a person for DUI to a 3 day alcohol education program (that dad paid for), but as a first degree misdemeanor, can be given up to a total sentence of six months that can be re-imposed upon a violation of probation.

Because of this, I felt he was likely to receive substantial jail time from both judges that they were not obligated to have run "concurrently" (at the same time). As separate offenses, they could give him close to a year in jail on the 2 crimes.

Another key in his decision making was my written assurance that there would be no more apartments, money, or other financial assistance provided. My advice, (that he was not obligated to follow) was to do whatever he felt would give him the best long-term chance at recovery and having a "life" when this was all over, if it ever would be! I was learning why so many other parents I had spoken with had decided to cut off their addicted children financially. I was surprised to learn how many, once they figured out that their continued assistance was actually prolonging their child's illness, allowed them to become homeless and live in a shelter!

CHAPTER 20

PACKING AND MOVING "THE STUFF"

One piece of advice I saw in the book *Setting Boundaries with Your Adult Children*, by Allison Bottke, was that you should not pack and move your adult addict's property when they get separated from it by their own actions (going to jail, etc). Experiencing the drastic consequence of losing all your personal effects sends a very powerful message. Despite this knowledge, as a parent, I continued my self-flagellation and arguable enabling by choosing to spend the money, time and effort packing and storing his personal property yet again. I felt guilt over allowing myself once again to be talked into the whole apartment idea, and would feel guilt knowing all of Ryan's things were disposed of, forcing him to start over!

So, for the nth time (nobody really remembers how many) I began the cumbersome work of packing up personal property, washing dishes, cleaning bathrooms, toilets and floors and throwing away trash (including needles and drug paraphernalia.) When I ran across the stash of needles he told me I would find, it was still, for me, a disgusting and terrifying shock to find these implements he had been using to inject this deadly substance into his veins and brain! (would this ever end short of a self-induced, early death?)

The apartment was, at least for my son and my past experiences with him, somewhat clean by his standards. He did call me from jail while I was working there. I mentioned to him that his bank statement was in the mail box and asked him if any of the Christmas money ($1,500 from my mother) was still left. He gulped and said "not much, maybe 15 bucks!" This was after 30 days.

So, 2 days later, after investing probably 8 to 10 hours of my labor (my 57 year old back was sore!), renting a truck and paying my brother-in-law to help me, I returned his "stuff" to the U-Haul storage facility I had taken it from 30 days before. My account would continue to be billed $55 per month. I did, however, lay down the law in writing that this would be the last time I would do this. "The next time this stuff gets moved is when you can rent the truck, have a license to drive it, a friend to help you move it, and an apartment you are renting with money you have earned from a job. The next time, if there is one, you are in this predicament, the landlord (or landfill) gets your stuff"!

CHAPTER 21

BACK TO JAIL

Over the next 3 weeks I received, almost daily, a collect call from Ryan at the jail. In nearly all of these calls was the anguish of not knowing how long he would be there. (Ryan had never been good at uncertainty. He did not have the patience for it and had always tried to exercise control over his circumstances and anyone who tried to control them (and him) became the enemy!) "What was the next step and when?", "Why can't the drug court and public defender get me out of here sooner, or at least tell me where I'm going next (and when)?"

One of the calls dealt with the anguish of receiving a summons to appear back in the Upper Arlington Mayor's Court for a probation revocation hearing. This is the court where Ryan was first charged with DUI in July, 2008. One of the conditions of that probation was that he not drink alcohol, use drugs, drive under the influence, or receive other charges for similar offenses.

The magistrate in that court has a reputation for being tough on repeat offenders and still had 177 days of jail time "on the shelf", meaning suspended time during probation and good behavior that could be re-imposed for a violation. Under Ohio law the judge is empowered to sentence a person for DUI to a 3 day alcohol education program (that dad paid for), but as a first degree misdemeanor, can be given up to a total sentence of six months that can be re-imposed upon a violation of probation.

The Franklin County Municipal Court Drug Court had told Ryan he would be kept in jail until they found an acceptable residential treatment program to send him to. When he became aware of his hearing on probation revocation in Upper Arlington, he also feared getting "slammed" by the Magistrate there. So, he toyed with the notion of dropping out of the drug court program, doing his time and having all of it (probation, jail, etc) over with.

All of this reasoning just goes to show how self-deluded a drug addict can get. His public defender told him that if he did this, he could count on significant jail time from both judges in the 2 courts. She also assured him that there was no requirement for these judges to sentence him "concurrently" (serving the sentences at the same time), and that they could each give him 6 months and, worst case, he could get close to a year. She explained that opting out of drug court would be a signal to both judges that he really wasn't trying to help himself, and they would deal more harshly with him.

Anyway, that was the end of that illogical thinking. Soon after this I received a call from the court asking me if I could check with my insurance and see if they would cover a program in Massillon, Ohio called Quest Recovery. This was a minimum 90 day residential program that had had some good track record of success in cases like Ryan's. What I learned was that the program was free to residents of that county (stark County, Ohio), but cost $76 per day for others. My insurance recognized the program but later determined it did not meet their requirements in certain regards (having professional drug counselors and the like- Quest's counselors are all recovering addicts, but more on this later).

They agreed to help Ryan for the small amount the insurance was willing to pay, and then to negotiate something with him to pay them back over time. I was pretty shocked to learn that a small county like Stark County would fund a program like this, but a larger city like Columbus had nothing similar.

Anyway, after much delay, and consternation for Ryan being locked up for another several weeks, there was finally a plan to get him into Quest. Then the big hurdle to cross was the UA Mayors' Court. Would they go for this, or would they send him to jail? Ryan attended his hearing in UA, where I acted as his attorney one more time (public defenders are not able to appear in a Mayor's Court, and discussed the plan with the Magistrate and Probation Officer there.

The UA Magistrate was ready to send him to jail for all of his non-complaince with their probation (which included a second DUI conviction). After I explained that Ryan was heroin addict, he said, with seemingly more sympathy, "Well, that's about as bad as it gets. IF he is really trying to help himself and this program is one he can't walk away from, I'm willing to give him one more chance to complete it successfully. Make sure he knows, though, that if he screws up again, I will drop kick his ass for the remaining 177 days I have on the shelf (the suspended portion of the sentence)!"

CHAPTER 22

QUEST RECOVERY-WILSON HALL

On March 14, I picked Ryan up at the jail and prepared to transport him to Quest, about 2 hours away. I was to pick him up at 9:00 am. As is typical, they delayed his release until around 10:00. At his request, I had brought some McDonald's food and Starbuck's Coffee. When he came out from his 25 days of confinement, I hugged him and said, "well, I guess your food and coffee will be cold". He replied, "do I look like I care?" Despite the 38 degree temperature, the sun was out. Uncharacteristically for my son, he remarked, "I'm just glad to be free, in the fresh air and the sun is shining!"

I went with him to the storage facility where we picked up several bags of clothing to take along. As is typical with addicts, his clothing was haphazardly stuffed in trash bags, with no sense of organization or sorting of any kind. On top of this, most had not been laundered. When we arrived at the facility, it took him about an hour and ½ to go through the 5 or 6 trash bags and pick out a couple weeks of clothing appropriate to the weather. (after getting back to Columbus, I stuffed the remaining clothes bags back into the U-Haul storage facility. I refused to sort, wash or otherwise handle the clothes. After all, who knew for how long I would still be paying to store this stuff?)

The staff at Quest seemed very nice and friendly. They assured me that Ryan would like it there, and that "there are many people here who want to help". They also predicted he would gain weight because "the food here is really good and you get a lot of it!" Ryan had been looking for a couple years like a refugee from a World War ll concentration camp. Heroin addicts typically do not eat, and it's about the lowest thing on their priority list. Their days are spent finding the money to buy their dope, then finding the dealer, then getting ready to do the whole thing again in 12 hours to avoid feeling dope sick! What a life!

The staff explained that it would be 2 ½ weeks before he would be eligible to receive a Saturday visit. I was also told to be prepared to not hear from him for a couple weeks. After I hugged him and told him I loved him I drove away looking at him in the rearview mirror

I closed my eyes and prayed, "God will this finally be the beginning of the end of this nightmare for Ryan and the rest of us. Your will be done". Only time would tell.

CHAPTER 23

MY FIRST VISIT TO QUEST

My first opportunity to visit Ryan at Quest came on Saturday April 3, 2011. Because Massillon is a 2 hour drive from Columbus, I had to leave home at 7:00 am. Quest requires on each visit that the visitor attend a family program" on addiction at 9 am, with the visit from 10 to 11:30. The program is a good addiction education programs for families, both to learn more about their family members' addiction, but also to understand what the program is trying to teach them.

As mentioned earlier, all the counselors at Quest are recovering addicts and the man leading the family education this first visit was a recovering heroin addict named Mr. Lancaster, who had 11 years of sobriety. He spoke from personal experience about the disease of addiction, what the addicts go through and that they all deal with many thinking distortions. I came away very impressed with this program, its quality and approach. I remember thinking "finally, maybe this was a real treatment program".

When I saw Ryan for the first time in 26 days, the first thing I was struck by was the dramatic change in his personal appearance in such a short time! He appeared to have gained perhaps 15 or 20 pounds. I had to blink and do a double take. I barely recognized him! His face, arms hands and neck looked so much fuller. His skin color and eyes looked great!

Gone were the sunken, dark eyes, the jaundiced look and the baggy pants falling half- way down his butt. He said he had been eating well and a lot, and that there were absolutely no drugs of any kind there, unlike CTC. He said that the 50 days he had been sober were the longest stretch without substances in the 4 ½ years since he left Midwest Academy!

Ryan went on to tell me that Quest was the first "real treatment program" he had ever attended, not a half-way house for convicted felons returning to the street, like CTC. There were AA meetings every day, and group counseling sessions. The other men there (only 22 to 24 at one time) all help work on each other to teach each other and themselves honesty and accountability. He told me at least 10 times how grateful he was that I came to see him.

Ryan was wearing a watch with an alarm that went off every hour, at which time he would recite the Serenity Prayer, pray to be healed, and change his life around. He told me he had had a revelation that he needed spiritual help to get well! Another change he told me of was that he was no longer depressed and was sleeping well at night. (Both of these had been long-standing problems for him for as many years as I could remember)

One of my big surprises was learning that Ryan had been working out. I had told Ryan for years that physical exercise was a great remedy for depression. He had always ridiculed this idea, telling me exercise was stupid and he had no interest in it. I said to him "who are you and what have you done to my son?"

Ryan had also written a letter to me that he shared with me, as follows:

"Dear Dad,

I am writing this to tell you things I wish I could say or wish I could have done. You have always been there for me, for better or worse, and done whatever you believed to be right to help me, for that I appreciate you and your love for me. But, I have a lot of resentments I keep in, too.. I blame you and mom for the way I was raised and what I grew up believing was important. You acknowledge the abuse my mother put us through, and I hate you for not saving me from it. I constantly told you how upset and emotionally distraught I was from my mother's treatment. Why did you allow it to go on? The negative beliefs and low self worth I feel constantly are a direct response to this emotional abuse (my belief). You could have stopped it. I resent the fact that you threw money at problems and I learned that there was a quick fix to anything. I used drugs to deal with my pain and problems. Drugs are bought and another type of quick fix. I was never taught to deal with my feelings or problems or how. You rescued me from consequence after consequence of my actions, teaching me I can manipulate my way out of consequences and most problematic situations for that matter. When I was young you pushed your religious beliefs on me. When I rejected them, you hurt me so bad with what you said I might never be able to forgive it (saying that I wasn't what you envisioned when I was born!) You are the only parent who ever made me feel better or have any self worth, and I felt rejected and worthless because of what you said. As I said, I appreciate your love and support, but you enabled me for years by giving me money. A place to stay, food, clothes, aka bare essentials were ok, but hundreds of dollars every few days? Come on, you helped me to kill myself slowly for years. I wish you could have seen that and stopped sooner. I love you dad, and I always will. Making you proud has always been a huge priority of mine. I just never have believed that to be possible, so why try when I know it's going to fail? That is changing every day and I can't wait to show you the person I am becoming. I understand I may sound like a victim, but I am just trying to vent my feeling and beliefs. I have tried to tell you this before, but you just call me a victim but I believe you do that to feel better about the guilt I know you feel. I also have the understanding that change is something I am responsible for. The way I was raised and the beliefs created are in the past and something I cannot change. I accept that it is my choice not to work on and change these beliefs, thoughts and feelings. I wish I could have "gotten it" sooner and acknowledged these issues. I wish I would have worked on and changed them, but it was easier to stay sick. Change only happens when the pain of staying the same outweighs the pain of change. I wish I hadn't spent the last few years doing nothing but killing myself. And not leading the kind of life you can be proud of. I wish I realized and wanted sobriety and a good, respectable life, like I do today, years ago."

A couple times during his reading of the letter, when recounting some of the problems he had with me, I interrupted to apologize and explain my actions. To this he said, "You don't have to apologize. I know you're sorry, but this is not about you. It's about me getting this off my chest so I can move on!"

2 weeks later, Ryan's mother went to visit him. On the voice mail she left me to describe the visit she said "He seems to be a changed young man". She actually seemed to want to go visit him again soon, despite the 6 ½ hours you need to invest on a Saturday to go there.

Over the next several weeks, I got multiple phone calls from Ryan. He continued to sound changed. When I said, one week, that neither I nor his mom could visit that week, he said "that's ok. I understand it's a long trip. I'd like to see you, but come when you can". What a change from the immature, self-centered kid I had come to know over the last 7 or 8 years! My hopes for a permanent change were growing. I knew, though, that I needed to temper these hopes with the reality I had heard from a year's attendance at Nar-Anon meetings. 93% of heroin addicts re-lapse. Permanence of sobriety in his age group is a shockingly low 7%!

Still, Ryan insisted that this was the first time he ever really wanted to get sober and stay that way. Even the day he arrived at Quest he told me he could not fathom the thought of life from age 22 on without getting high. He said then that he didn't like the way he felt sober! Now he was saying that he never knew how great it felt to be sober. I could only hope and pray that that he might find a permanent healthy, well-adjusted feeling he had never felt since he started doing drugs at age 13!

CHAPTER 24

A GREAT PROGRAM

Over the next 4 months or so, I visited Ryan at Quest several times. Every time, I left more impressed with the quality of the program there and the metamorphosis that seems to be happening with my son. He was reading the "Big Book", *Alcoholics Anonymous* and I continued to see a changed person. He attended multiple AA meetings and other counseling sessions per day and was really working on his spiritual side. He told me he was praying and giving gratitude every hour, and the counselors seemed to be doing wonderful things with him. They were holding him accountable and working on his perception flaws daily. One of the things he learned was that acceptance was the answer to all his problems and that "nothing happens in God's world by mistake".

About this time, I received a call from Ryan and his counselor, whom he really had high regard for. They mentioned that he had been working on his "exit plan", and that he had to have someplace to live once he got out. I had been encouraging him to see if there was any way he could stay in the Massillon area, find a place to live and become employed. It seemed to me he had really made some connections in that community, had been attending local AA meetings and had a sponsor there. I was really concerned that if he came back to the Columbus area, he could fall in with some of the old "friends" he had associated with in the past, basically his "drug buddies" from high school.

One of the adages you learn in treatment, AA and Al Anon is that for an addict to stay sober, they need to change the "people, places and things" in their lives. Despite this, Ryan seemed dead set on coming "back home". The explanation I heard from the counselor was that Ryan wanted to come back, and that there were basically 3 options. He wanted my opinion on them. He said Ryan could either live with me, with his mother, or in a halfway house that would cost some money, perhaps $100 per week, and that after a couple weeks where he would need help paying for it, he could be working and paying his own way.

I told him I could not take the risk of his coming into my home, particularly with my 9 year old daughter there, whom my wife and I were committed to shielding from some of the negativity that had been a big part of life with Ryan in the past and could occur again based upon the odds of staying sober we had learned. Ryan also had some pretty significant emotional issues that (in my opinion) he had inherited, or at the very least learned from the environment he had grown up in with his mother. After he told me his mom was willing to let him stay there for awhile, I told him this also was risky to him, in my opinion. He had always fought with her and I felt her own depression and negativity would not be a good influence on him. To his vast disappointment, I told them both that I voted for the halfway house, although I knew I was not in control (was powerless) over what he did.

Despite this, he made an agreement with his mother to come and stay there for three months while he got on his feet. There were also some other guidelines she laid down for him, household rules, behavioral expectations and the like.

Shortly before leaving Quest in June, his mom and I were both invited to a "graduation" ceremony at Quest. This was really touching and meaningful, as all the other Quest residents got to stand up and tell Ryan what was in their hearts about him and give him their best wishes. A common theme was that most of them had had kind of a negative first impression of him. They thought he was a "know it all", cocky and spoiled, that he had had everything handed to him. They called him a "big city kid" who thought he was a hot shot.

Some of the Counselors gave a personal message to Ryan at the Graduation ceremony. One of them, Mr. Lancaster (whom I had gotten to know during the visits and respected a lot) told Ryan "I am terribly afraid for you". Mr. Lancaster is a recovering heroin addict who has been clean for 20 years. However, he knew the risks associated with the disease, especially for someone so young. Mr. Hewitt, Ryan's personal counselor, got up and said that Ryan was so smart and knowledgeable about addiction that he could be a counselor himself someday.

What I did not hear until about 9 months later was that Mr. Hewitt had also told him the following." What you are about to do in going back to the same City you lived in before, and not changing the people, places and things in your life is very dangerous for you. Not having a sober social network in place when you leave rehab is like getting all your training, equipment, weapons and so forth in the military and then being dropped alone behind enemy lines with nobody to help you survive"!

CHAPTER 25

BACK UNDER MOM'S ROOF!

Despite all my fears and the advice of Ryan's counselors, he came back to our home town of Columbus, Ohio in late June 2011, and moved in with Melinda. At the start of this part of his journey, he seemed to be doing well. My daughter invited him to walk with her in the July 4th parade in Dublin, Ohio along with her swimming team and he readily and happily agreed. We saw this as a good sign, since in the past part of Ryan's "victim" speech (whenever he wanted to get something from me: time attention, but usually money) he launched into this whole speech about how I cared more for my "new happy little family" than I did for him; spent more of my time and attention on them. He would also say he was the "black sheep of the family" and that I was embarrassed by him. So, Ryan seeming so willing to be with us felt like a great sign of change.

These positive signs, however, were short-lived, and soon (within a week or 2 literally), I started to see signs of potential problems popping up in my son's life. The first thing I noticed, within days of his coming home, was his reporting to me that he was seeing Trent (the first kid he smoked dope with in high school) and several other former friends, all of whom had been drug-using buddies of the past. He rationalized this by saying that all these friends were now "clean" and had learned their lessons, were attending AA, and doing other positive things in their lives.

He also starting seeing a girl he had dated a few times in high school named Monica, who I later learned "had been a heroin addict but was also clean" and he was going to NA meetings with her and the others.

I don't know for sure how many NA or AA meetings Ryan attended, but I am pretty sure it was fewer than 5 over the 9 months following his return home to Columbus! About the same time Ryan also complained about living with his mom, saying she was "crazy', treated him like a little kid and that they were fighting a lot. Occasionally I heard from her also about his disrespect, failure to keep the house clean, and constant demands for rides here and there and occasional money. Ryan was also asking me for rides, and often they were to see friends and go get cigarettes.

I also was hearing Ryan talk about the fact that he was drinking beer "occasionally, but only a couple here and there", and that this shouldn't be a problem as he "had never had a problem with alcohol and didn't even like the taste of it that much", therefore he would not abuse it. A couple times I gave him some money to go out on a date, since he told me he was lonely for female companionship and despite his best efforts had not yet been able to find a job in the bad economy. He also told me how some employers had turned him down for a job because his court records still showed that his DUI case was still open and nobody would hire him until it said it was closed.

I had experienced in the past Ryan saying he couldn't find a job and it was always, in my mind questionable how hard he was really trying. On this particular trip home he found a job quickly at a local deli but within a week or 2 reported that they "were not giving him enough hours" so he decided to look elsewhere. (I suspect there was more to this story but decided not to challenge him on it). After that, no other good job prospect seemed to come up despite his "trying as hard as I can" to find work. He had opportunities to work through 2 local temporary agencies, but refused, basically to work. His reasoning was that he needed to be available when they called him and he did not have a car.

Other previous "patterns" came up over the next several months:

1. Frequent requests for rides to see friends (always "former" drug users.

2. Reports of his staying out very late and sleeping most of the following day.
3. Many reasons why employment was elusive.
4. Increasingly frequent requests for money or other financial support.

CHAPTER 26

FALLING APART AND GOING "BACK OUT"

The next 6 months were characterized by Ryan continuing to slide down the slippery slope of addiction once again, although I didn't recognize it all at once. When he came back home, he was again placed into the Drug court program, which came with a daily requirement to call in for random drug tests and attend a Friday court session.

Some weeks I gave him rides to these meetings. He nearly always wanted a ride somewhere to a questionable part of town afterwards, and was by now frequently asking for money again. The amounts of his "need" kept increasing and soon I slipped back into my familiar patterns of lecturing him, but in the end giving him larger and larger sums of money.

I still had little communication with his mother, based upon the bad blood lingering from the divorce that was by his time almost 6 years in the past. When I did talk to her, she constantly complained of his disrespect, and his absolute refusal to keep his living space clean. She also complained of his asking her for money and, when we compared notes, it seemed he was using the same explanations for his "need" for money to both us, therefore doubling his take.

We had many of the same yelling matches and arguments that previously had characterized our interactions, but as usual, I gave in to his requests most of the time. I was seriously back into the insanity but kept deluding myself with beliefs that he had been staying up late, going to nightclubs and buying drinks for women. One time, he said he had been drinking and that this seemed to be getting out of control, both in frequency and amount.

I told him I had no responsibility to buy drinks for his lady friends, and after more promises were made to change (and a denial of drug use), I would give in again and pass out the cash. He also told me he had gotten a prescription to Tramadol, which he described as a non-narcotic pain killer. He needed this, he said, for the pain of a broken hand. He suffered the broken hand when a friend told him he could punch a motorcycle helmet with those special protective gloves and not get hurt. (I couldn't make up this stuff, really!)

Shortly after Christmas of 2011, Ryan informed me he was no longer going to attend the weekly Drug Court meetings on Friday and also was tired of calling in every day for the possibility of a drug test. I figured at this point that if he was considered a probation violator, he would be arrested again and some of the madness would stop.

In February, he decided he might need another rehab, for alcohol and Tramadol this time, not heroin. His friend Trent told him of a program in Cleveland he had attended a couple times, called Glenbeigh. Ryan liked the sound of it as it was a hospital affiliated program and, I believe, sounded cushy and not demanding. Health insurance was accepted and Trent told him they "do not make you pay the difference" between what the insurance pays and what it actually costs. Trent still had a significant debt to them for his two trips there, was not paying it back and there were no consequences.

Ryan therefore contacted Glenbeigh and made his own application to go there. They accepted him. I think he was actually just running from the Drug Court and probation violations.

CHAPTER 27

GLENBEIGH

On March 12, 2012, Ryan got the call that they were ready to take him at Glenbeigh. He seemed very excited to be going and told me he was really tired of living the way he had been. He really wanted to get off the Tramadol, and "everything else")! I was unsure what the everything else referred to, but I learned in Nar-Anon not to ask, because it's really none of my business.

I stopped over to his mom's house to say goodbye to him and he told me, in retrospect, he had made a huge mistake in returning to Columbus after leaving Wilson Hall in July of 2011. He had made a whole new group of friends while in Massillon, Ohio, in effect a "sober support network" that he left when he came back home. He had been lonely and the only people he knew at home were his former drug friends.

As had been the case so many times before, (and many "rehabs" before), Ryan's time at Glenbeigh had barely begun when he started calling me saying he didn't think this was the right place for him. His first several days were marked by sickness and withdrawal, which was expected. I believe, in retrospect, that his decision to go there was largely influenced by his friend, Trent in Columbus, who had been a patient at Glenbeigh several times. From conversations with Trent, Ryan no doubt came to the conclusion that since this was a hospital they would be able to give him medications to ease the withdrawal symptoms. This did not end up being the case. (My strongly held opinion at this point in my "experience" tells me that anything that eases the symptoms will not help the addict experience what he or she really needs, which is to feel the pain.

In any event, the calls wanting out started within a couple days. I learned a new concept, talking to one of the counselors there, and that dealt with the notion that addicts can have chronic withdrawal syndrome, that lasts beyond the 5 or 6 days it normally takes to get "off" heroin. Sometimes these lingering, chronic symptoms can last weeks, months or even years, depending upon how long the addict has been using, and how much. It seems in the case of my son, the extent of the using was pretty severe even though he was only 23 years old!

Anyway, there was a big "roller coaster" of positives and negatives about this rehab experience. On the positive side, he related conversations with a roommate at the hospital who was in his late 50s who said he was just like Ryan, in that his father had plenty of money, and enabled his addiction for many years. He told Ryan, "you need to change your approach now, because you don't want to end up like me in 30 years-still addicted, going through hell and rehab!" The guy's life had basically been ruined as he could not hold down a job, have a family or do any of the things most people aspire to. Ryan was telling me he prayed with this gentleman and had a spiritual experience and he would never do drugs again!

On the other side of the ledger, he kept telling me he didn't like Glenbeigh, they weren't helping him and he could make it the rest of the way on his own. After some probing, I found out that he was being told he should have fully withdrawn in the first 5 or 6 days and they could do nothing more for him. However, he claimed to still be experiencing some pretty severe sickness and "just wanted to leave." When he first checked into this facility, his plan had been to go from there to a "three quarter's way house", where he could work, go to AA meetings and be in a sober living environment. Now, he was telling me the waiting lists for these were too long, and he could find a place to go on his own faster.

The bottom line to all this was that he had me talk to his counselor on the phone and she told me Ryan was "leaving the facility against medical advice", and there was nothing they could do. She also encouraged me to "cut him off" financially, because she feared he would start using again. Ryan said he agreed, but needed a little "seed money" to get started, find a job, etc. And, as usual, I gave in to this request, wanting desperately to help him, hoping he had found his bottom and really needed some financing for basic living expenses!

I later learned (a few months down the road, as usual), that he bought heroin and used the day he walked out of Glenbeigh. A pattern had been emerging: Ryan always revealed these things to me later on at another low point in his experience with drug addiction. When he made these revelations it was always coupled with a new "low", where he had "hit bottom and would never use again" Part of his recovery, he would say, required "scrupulous honesty", as they teach in AA. These revelations were also coupled with promises to never do it again, a request to "cut me off" as that is the "only way I can make it", but always needing "just a little bit more money" to get him through to his self-sufficiency!

CHAPTER 28

MOVING TO CANTON

About the time Ryan returned from Glenbeigh, he discovered that there was a warrant out for him for violating probation in the Franklin County Municipal Court drug court program. Since, January, he had been skipping his daily calls he was required to make, and also failing to appear at the required Friday morning court appearance, checking in with the Probation Officer and other requirements of this program. What I found out later explained why: he had relapsed somewhere around Christmas time of 2011.

Coincidentally about the time he learned of the warrant, he started talking about moving to the Massillon, Ohio area where he had developed the "sober network" while in the Quest Wilson Hall program. Looking back, the reality behind this "life decision" was to get away from Franklin County, where the possibility of Probation violation and there fore jail hung over his head.

Applying himself for one of the first times I had seen, he quickly located a room for rent in Canton, Ohio, close to Massillon. It was being rented for $200 per month, utilities included, by 2 ladies, Tina and Nancy. Ryan spoke to them and reported to me that he was being "lead by God" to this situation. The price was right, and the ladies had told him "no drugs or alcohol" on the premises was their policy. Ryan always had contended that situations like this where there was "forced sobriety" would really help him!

Once this arrangement was established, I was again asked for financial support until Ryan could find a job and take over these responsibilities himself. I agreed, again wanting to believe he was on the right track and doing this for the right reasons.

As had happened on numerous prior occasions, it just seemed very difficult for Ryan to find a job. He talked continually to me by phone about having this or that great job lead, and then nothing ever happened. Thus the need for financial assistance continued. He also would show up in Columbus (or very close to Columbus) on weekends. He would call me and ask if we could get together for lunch, then always ask for money for gas or something else (clothing needed for job interviews, a set of special protective clothing for a job he had been offered at a factory where one of his sober friends worked and put in a good word for him. He even told me he was going on weekend camping trips with his sober group of friends, needed a tent, sleeping bag, etc!)

Why did I not get suspicious, and why did I continue to come through with financial support is beyond me. Even when it seemed he was always spending time on weekends with his friend, Trent (or other previous drug acquaintances, I continually said "yes" to these requests, all the while lecturing him on the cost of traveling to and from Columbus, and the need to stay in Canton to stay close to the sober people!

I later found out he was asking his mom for money at the same time, and getting it, telling many of the same stories. I continued not communicating with her based upon my strong desire to avoid these uncomfortable conversations!

CHAPTER 29

JUNE 18, 2012 BACK TO JAIL!

On Monday June 18, some events were transpiring that I found out about early that evening. I received a call from an "unknown" number. It was Ryan, who, in a very somber voice asked me if I "knew anything". I said "no" and he said "well, I'm in jail".

Unknown to me, he had stayed over night in Columbus after coming down from Canton for another weekend trip. I had been told that he was supposed to work at his new factory job on Monday, and that he had also been scheduled to work Saturday and Sunday. It always seemed these work schedules were changing and giving him the opportunity to make a trip to Columbus, because he was lonely and hated Canton. On this particular occasion he had told me he thought he had "bed bugs" and planned to throw away the second hand mattress the ladies had given him to use, and need to come to Columbus to get his mattress out of storage. I had gotten him this mattress for his last apartment in the fall of 2010, prior to his relapse in the Winter of 2011.

Anyway, these were the facts that lead to his being taken to jail. It seems he was at Trent's house smoking some of "that legal pot substitute", and Trent's brother called the police on them. They discovered he had an outstanding warrant and took him to jail. At this point, he told me he was really afraid he would lose his home with Tina and Nancy in Canton.

The net result of this was spending about 12 days in jail in Columbus, where he was going through withdrawal and, by his reports, vomiting and defecating on himself and being put into isolation for "observation". When he finally went back before the Judge of the Drug court, he was dismissed from the Drug Court Program and told his "Probation was over". He felt like he was home "Scott free", and was happy about this. I was infuriated!

Because I was unwilling to pick him up at jail, he arranged to have Trent's father pick him up and return him back to Trent's mother's home where his car had been left after the arrest. Trent's dad called me, agreed to pick Ryan up, and even gave him a tank of gas. I had told Ryan he was "cut off" from my financial support, and it was up to him to figure out what to do and where to go from there!

Inexplicably in my mind, instead of returning immediately to Canton, he stayed 3 nights at Trent's dad's house before going back. (See how many "red flags" I chose to ignore). He then returned to Canton, and was able, in his words, "to throw himself on Tina and Nancy's mercy" by telling them he had now hit bottom and would be resuming his sober life with his network there. (Ryan, and probably every other addict, is an extremely skillful manipulator and liar!) While they scolded him for lying to them, they took compassion on him and vowed to try to help him.

At this point, he told me he had lined up a new job working in a health club, and wanted me to give him some money to get a one-year membership there to start working out. Is anyone surprised to learn I said "yes"? He always has been able to appeal to me based upon things I want to hear, in this case his desire to get healthy and work to support himself!

CHAPTER 30

DAD CHECKING UP

This time I felt I made a big breakthrough in my own resolve to no longer pay for drugs for this kid! I had saved Jim's (Trent's Dad's) phone number in my cell when he called to inform me he was picking Ryan up at jail. Ultimately Ryan persuaded me to give him a hundred bucks to get re-established. However, my distrust led me to call Tina and Nancy and asked them to "keep me informed" about Ryan's activities, especially concerning his job and any extended absences from their home. They agreed to this. I also called Trent's dad, and got his agreement (after telling him my concerns) to call me and let me know if he showed up there.

Around July 11th, Tina called and said Ryan was doing "very well" and that she and Nancy "loved him like a son". They were willing to help him any way they could, as long as he stayed off drugs and was honest with them. They also mentioned in this call that he had left their home for a couple days to stay over in Massillon with a "sober friend", and start attending AA meetings again. (This story immediately roused my suspicions that something else was up!)

On the 13th, almost as if "on cue", Jim called and said Ryan had stayed at his home in Columbus the previous night. He said Ryan and Trent "had smoked some grass" but beyond this had done nothing wrong. (Trent's dad had always, in my opinion, taken a much more lax

99

attitude toward marijuana than I had, believing it was just something kids in this age group do, never mind that his own son was also a heroin addict.) Jim told me he had lectured Ryan about "hard drugs" and advised him to go back to Canton and stay away from Columbus.

I was apopleptic, knowing I had been had! Ryan had committed to me that he would stay in Canton and get his life back on track. I called Tine after this and informed her of where Ryan had really gone. The land ladies were also concerned because they said Ryan had not been working or looking for work, and had been "holed up" in his room, not answering the door or his phone after he returned.

I spoke with Ryan about all this the following day and he denied doing anything other than smoking "some of that *legal* pot-like substance" He swore he was "clean" and had a conversation with the land ladies about all this. He also said he was waiting for the gym to call him back about starting work and felt that would happen any day. He mentioned it was run by an uncle of one of his sober friends, who was sympathetic to addicts who were struggling to remain clean. (being a recovering alcoholic himself). It would not be long until "all hell broke loose" again!

Later the next day, after convincing the ladies he was still clean, Ryan called to tell me he was in Mercy Hospital in Canton, having had a seizure. (The last seizure he had was related to Benzo withdrawal). He denied this was the issue this time. He said he had gone to the main offices of Quest Recovery (who ran Wilson Hall in Massillon, to apply for their Intensive Out Patient (IOP) program. While taking the assessment, he had the seizure. He was uncertain as to why, and said the hospital thought he may have a seizure disorder.

Tine went to see Ryan at the hospital, as it was near their home. After reassuring her that he was ok, he told her he would be home shortly. He also had told me he was fine, and would be leaving the hospital shortly.

That evening, while in Tina's home, he became argumentative and struggled physically with Tina, apparently kicking her in the stomach. (He later related to me that he did this while having another seizure, which Tina told me was not true.) I was on a business trip in Pittsburgh, and received a call from Tina around midnight, telling me

Ryan was in the hospital, and was "extremely high on something", and saw an empty bottle of pills. She didn't know if he had tried to kill himself with an overdose or not, but she feared for his life. She also said that, although she was really worried about him, she and Nancy had resolved to kick him out based upon his abusive behavior. She said she could not tolerate this behavior in her home.

While Ryan was in the hospital, the ladies packed up all his belongings and stuffed them into his car. When he returned to their home they told him he was kicked out. He pleaded with them to reconsider and to give him another chance. They refused. He called me desperately pleading for me to take him in, as he had nowhere else to go and only $14 to his name. As difficult as it was for me as a father, I finally got up the fortitude to tell him he was on his own. I told him to go back to Quest and check himself in to their Crisis Center.

(I later found out from the people at Quest that when Ryan came there the day all this happened, he had asked to get into their Methadone program, and insisted upon getting a dose of Methadone immediately. They told him he needed an assessment first and that's when he had the seizure. It had been drug induced by taking a large dose of some kind of medication!)

CHAPTER 31

32 DAYS IN A DIFFERENT JAIL

The following day I was returning home from me trip to Pittsburgh when I received a call around noon from a State Patrolman in Richland County, Ohio near Mansfield. He told me he had Ryan in custody and that he had been involved in an accident along Interstate 71 near Mansfield. This made it obvious based upon the location that he was trying to return to Columbus. The patrolman said nobody was hurt and asked if I would be willing to come and get him if they determined after some tests, that he was not intoxicated. Again, I gritted my teeth, swallowed hard and said "no".

A couple hours later the patrolman called back and said Ryan was being taken to the County jail. He had been charged with a DUI (his 3rd), and "hit-skip" (for bumping into a car and then trying to drive away....)

Ryan pleaded "no contest" to the new charges and did not ask for a Public Defender. He was found guilty on the charges and given a jail sentence of 180 days, with 120 suspended, 30 days of which was mandatory time under Ohio law. He also received a 2 year driver's license suspension until July, 2014.

Over the next couple of weeks I accepted some collect calls from him in jail. Again for the umpteenth time, the truth began to slowly come out. Ryan admitted he had never really applied for a job while in Canton. He also never attended AA meetings or reunited with his sober friends. His weekend trips were for the purpose of buying heroin, which was cheaper in Columbus and more readily available, plus he manipulated me and his mother for money.

After getting through withdrawal again in jail (for the 3rd time "cold turkey"), he flatly asserted his desire to get back into rehab, stay clean and start over again. He even began to say that the whole series of events was planned by God to get him to this point, and that he was grateful for everything that had happened. He said there "were no accidents" and that he was reading the bible and praying every day. He was very humble and apologetic.

He told me that the day he went into the Quest center, he had been wandering the streets looking for a liquor store, hoping to find something that would alleviate his dope sickness for awhile. When he stumbled on the Quest offices by accident, he thought he would see if he could get some Methadone. It was true that they told him he needed an assessment to qualify for the Methadone Program.

The first seizure he claimed was as a result of taking 4200 mgs of some anti seizure medication he had gotten prescribed, and that hoped it would mitigate the withdrawal symptoms he was experiencing (Ryan had always been very good at researching and self-medicating, manipulating doctors, etc). The remaining events involving the land ladies, he still claims not to remember and believes they occurred during a seizure. Despite it all, he said getting to Quest, getting kicked out, and arrested and sent to jail was all part of God's plan for his recovery.

Ryan then started on a mission to get himself out of jail in Mansfield as soon as his first 30 days were up, and to get back into Quest's Wilson Hall program in Massillon, the program where he had experienced his best success back in the first half of 2011. It turned out that, because he had established the residence in Canton (Stark County), Wilson Hall could accept him into their program, which was taxpayer funded in Stark County. (Another part of God's overall plan, he believed).

Despite my resolve to detach myself from Ryan's life, I reluctantly agreed to make some phone calls, facilitate an assessment for this program, after the Richland County Probation officer said Ryan would not have much opportunity in jail to do this for himself. He also said he thought Ryan really needed "treatment, not jail". After 32 days of being locked up, choked unconscious and beaten up (a broken finger and ribs), I agreed to pick him up and transport him back to Wilson Hall.

CHAPTER 32

WILSON HALL II, AUGUST, 2012

I delivered Ryan back to Wilson Hall in mid-August. My early calls from him (after about 3 weeks there) revealed that he had a plan for what to do after his completion of the program. Instead of returning to Columbus (which he said had been a big mistake in 2011), he told me he was resolved to stay in Wilson Hall's Transition Program, which was upstairs in the same facility. He told me there was also a program he had already applied for and been accepted into, that would pay his living expenses while in Transition, and also provide him with assistance in job searching, resume writing and interviewing skills, as well as provide bus passes for transportation.

I went to visit him after 4 weeks and, as before, he looked great, looked healthy and had his color back. He had gained about 40 pounds since going to jail in Mansfield. He told me about how much he loved the program and was working on his "spiritual side" again. He also had re-connected with his sponsor in AA, and resumed the meetings he had attended prior to leaving Wilson Hall in July, 2011. He got tearful when he said that he knew he had to stay clean this time, and that if he relapsed again, he knew he would die.

CHAPTER 33
ESTABLISHING A NEW LIFE

I was skeptical and worried when Ryan told me he wanted to leave the safety of Wilson Hall, get a job and start living on his own. The good part about this decision was his seeming commitment not to return to Columbus, but to take up residence in Canton, which was just next door to Massillon. He had a couple options for doing this.

One was Wilson Hall's "transitional housing", where he could live in the upstairs part of the same building, at no cost, continue to have meals provided, and have access to all the same meetings, etc. that he had while in the residential program. The other option would be to move to Canton to a "sober house" called Phoenix House, where he could get a grant to pay for a couple months, then he would be on his own. Obviously, I was thinking the first option was better. He would have everything paid for and access to the sobriety programs Wilson Hall had to offer.

Ryan chose the Phoenix House option, because it gave him more freedom and was closer to where the jobs were located, in Canton. Not having a car or driver's license for the time being put him in a difficult spot, but this was part of the consequences of his choices and he seemed to get that for the first time. He moved into a house with 7 or 8 other men who were supposedly all sober, and working not only on staying that way, but working, earning a living and getting on with life.

Within a week, he landed a part time job at McDonald's making the minimum wage. This seemed acceptable in the short run, as his expenses were low, he had a food stamp card. Transportation was basically the bus and walking, but he seemed accepting of this. I was not financially supporting him anymore, and I was convinced it had to be that way in order for him to have a chance to make it. (How long did it take me to get around to that conclusion?)

In my conversations with him he seemed happy. He told me he was attending approximately 5 or 6 AA meetings per week, had reconnected with his sponsor, Bob, and felt things were going well. He was seeking some female companionship, an experience which, he said, had been "on hold" for many months. The first couple experiences there were not so good. Though they said they understood his situation, the 2 women he met first were both into partying and getting high (or drunk), despite telling Ryan they were only moderate in their usage. Neither of these situations lasted long, and I was surprised and pleased that he was mature and stable enough to let them go without the extreme emotional reactions that had characterized most of Ryan's previous "breakups"!

Ryan did come home for Christmas and told me just coming into Columbus made him extremely anxious, based upon past experience here. He also said spending time at his mother's house was hard, with all the memories of the last relapse and being around the drinking which was going on there over the holidays. When I took Ryan back to Canton the day after Christmas, he asked me to attend an AA meeting with him, which I did.

I was very moved by the experience and recommend it strongly to the parent of any addict going through what I went through. The camaraderie and love in the room is hard to forget, and I could see why this experience is so important to the prospect of staying sober. I was very impressed with the quality of relationships Ryan had forged in his time in Massillon and Canton.

It seems obvious to me now why they say to stay sober you need to change the "people, places and things" in your life. In Columbus, as Ryan has now attested, all of his friends were drug users. He now says they were not real friends, just people who used him for rides, money, drugs, etc. Real friends would not support you in doing things that risk your life, just because misery loves company. In Canton/Massillon, nearly all of Ryan's friends and acquaintances are recovering addicts and alcoholics. They are all in the same boat, trying to help each other live quality, happy, safe lives. What a difference this makes.

It wasn't long (about a month), before Ryan said he didn't like McDonald's. they gave him the "shit work", it was not full time and the wages were too low! I thought, "here we go again", this was a "pattern" (becoming dissatisfied at work, wanting to quit). One of the biggest differences now was I was not volunteering to support him financially and he finally was taking pride in making his own way.

What was different this time was that he soon found another job by leveraging a relationship he had in AA. One of his friends worked at a place called VXI Technologies where they did customer service for AT&T cell phone customers. Ryan applied there and was able to get hired despite his record and past. He decided "honesty was the best policy" about his drug problem. They made him furnish evidence of his rehab program and sobriety. Ultimately it may have boiled down to having a friend there who was a reliable employee and vouched for him.

Anyway, it was a full time job, with hourly wages between $9 and $14 per hour, depending upon performance, and advancement potential. It required 3 months of intense training, which is meant to wash out the unreliable and not -so- dedicated worker (which in my experience would have described my son to a tee). Anyway, he prevailed through the training and seems to be a "natural" in this job. He has always been very good with technology.

Ryan was able to secure his own apartment for around $425 per month with rent and utilities. It is not the best part of town, but it's within walking distance of work. I did relent and help him move his stuff out of storage and up to Canton at my expense. This did get me off the hook of having to pay about $60 per month for his storage, and I made clear that if he loses his apartment due to a relapse, or loses his job, I am not coming back to clean up the situation.

He is paying his own bills now and is saving money. It's the first time in his life and he's almost 25! He wants to get his license back and get a car, which he will pay for himself. He is dating a nice young lady with a Master's degree who is a teacher and a 5 years' sober recovering alcoholic. He is still, as of this writing, attending many weekly AA meetings and has an ambition to become a drug and alcohol counselor to help others like himself. (They say one of the best ways to stay in recovery is to "give your recovery away!)

It is now April of 2013 and Ryan just reached the milestone of 9 months sober. I don't know and have no control over, whether he will remain sober or relapse. The most important aspect of this, for me at this point, is that only he can control where he goes from here. As his sponsor, Bob, said when I attended another AA meeting with Ryan last month "to drink is to die" for him.

Another poignant story I heard lately was from another grieving mother at a Nar-Anon meeting who went to see a drug counselor for advice on what she could do to help her heroin- addicted son. He told her very directly "you act as if there's a Plan B that you, as a parent, have some influence over". "There is only Plan A for the addict. They either get sober on their own, or they die. It's that simple!"

CHAPTER 34

RYAN'S "LEAD"

On the one-year anniversary of Ryan beginning his "recovery", I was invited to attend an AA meeting in Massillon, Ohio, where Ryan was asked to "Lead". Basically a Lead is where the addict tells his story to the whole group. It's an honor they do not bestow on someone until they have at least one year in sobriety, but I learned it is unusual for a person's first Lead to occur on their first anniversary date.

I decided I couldn't miss this experience, and drove to Canton, and took Ryan and his girlfriend out to dinner beforehand. She is a recovering alcoholic with 5 years of sobriety under her belt. She's a very fine person who understands what Ryan has gone through and continues to go through.

Ryan felt honored but was nervous thinking about getting up in front of everyone to share his most personal stories. He told me that the advice he had gotten from others was not to prepare your remarks, but pray for assistance and then the words that come to you standing at the podium will be the messages God wants your audience to hear from you.

They started the meeting off, as usual with a reading from the Alcoholic's Anonymous "Big Book", and quoting How it Works. It is an interesting thing to hear, so I have quoted it here:

"Rarely have we seen a person fail who has thoroughly followed our path. Those who do not recover are people who cannot or will not completely give themselves to this simple program, usually men and women who are constitutionally incapable of being honest with themselves. These are such unfortunates. They are not at fault; they seem to have been born that way. They are naturally incapable of grasping and developing a manner of living which demands rigorous honesty. Their chances are less than average. There are those, too, who suffer from grave emotional disorders, but many of them to recover if they have the capacity to be honest.

Our stories disclose in a general way what we used to be like, what happened, and what we are like now. If you have decided you want what we have and are willing to go to any length to get it-than you are ready to take certain steps.

At some of these we balked. We thought we could find an easier, softer way. But we could not. With all the earnestness at our command, we beg of you to be fearless and thorough from the very start. Some of us have tried to hold on to our ideas and the result was nil until we let go absolutely.

Remember that we deal with alcohol (or drugs, or addiction)-cunning, baffling, powerful! Without help it is too much for us. But, there is One who has all the power-that one is God. May you find Him now!

Half measure availed us nothing. We stood at the turning point. We asked for his protection and care with complete abandon.

Here are the steps we took, which are suggested as a program of recovery:"

Then The Twelve Steps follow, exactly the same today as when AA was founded in 1939.

Bob, Ryan's sponsor and good friend introduced him to give his Lead, which I know was special to him. Ryan began by saying that "I didn't do anything under my own power to get sober". He attributed the way things turned out to guidance from God that showed up in how everything unfolded one year before.

He began by relating some information from his childhood. He told how he had been compared unfavorably to his sister growing up and was told how she never did some of the things Ryan had done and "why can't you be more like her". He attributed this to his mother. He also mentioned that we had moved around a lot while he was growing up (4 times by the time he got to high school) and that he "never felt part of anything" as a result of changing schools and friend so often.

Ryan related his first experience with alcohol "cherry sherry" at a friend's house when he was 14, and how good it made him feel. He told the story of lighting the "porta johns" on fire just to see what would happen, and getting caught and charged after burning them down. He got the charges dismissed for paying restitution (paid by his dad), so there were "never any real consequences in that situation or many others as I had paid lawyers and bailed him out of almost all the trouble he got into over the next several years.

He described the cruel treatment his mom gave him, how she told him "I hate you" and "you're the devil" on several occasions when she was angry with him. He further described how his mother would ground him, then he would talk me into letting him off the hook and how this would create fights between his parents. This also began a long term strategy of pitting one parent against the other.

Although Ryan said he liked the feeling alcohol gave him, when he got into high school he listened to upper classmen describe how much fun they were having getting "high". He said "I was always a thinker and a researcher" and decided to read everything he could get his hands on about drugs, their dangers and effects. The result was that he concluded marijuana was safe and planned out his first high which he did by himself. He enjoyed it so much, he concluded "I am going to do this for the rest of my life". For the first time, he felt relief and happiness from the misery he felt in life. From then on, he said, he made his body "a guinea pig", and set out to "try every drug there was."

He related the story of his grandfather dying of cancer and his not being able to attend from the drug sickness. He also talked about the 14 juvenile charges (12 misdemeanors and 2 felonies) that were plea bargained to 2 minor misdemeanors and probation with the help of a lawyer I had paid for. Again, no real consequences.

Ryan described how his trip to Hazelden was the start of his "going in and out of 8 different treatment programs" and how a probation officer gave him the choice of going to the juvenile lockup or to a foster home after he repeatedly skipped school and was failing. As he told the story, his parents decided to have him escorted to a disciplinary boarding school in Iowa for a year. This he said was not a treatment program, but gave him a "Daily reprieve" if he didn't violate the rules which were all aimed at teaching discipline only.

He related his choice to leave this program when he turned 18 and could no longer be held there. Within 2 weeks of his return to Columbus he was, as he said "off and running drinking and drugging with the same old friends". He told about how he had ever tried heroin and how his "Best friend", Trent put the needle in his arm for the first time. After he felt this experience, he settled on this as his drug of choice. At this point, he stated that his drug use was to help him control his emotions which were out of control and described himself as a "professional, emotional, chemical manipulator". He then said that heroin "took me down quicker than anything else" that he "separated drugs from alcohol" in his mind. He felt he could control alcohol use, but not heroin use.

He talked about his 3 DUI charges, and drug paraphernalia charges, and how he showed up drunk for the Mothers Against Drunk Driving (MADD) impact panel where victims come in and tell their stories, and getting kicked out of the session! He also admitted that while he always thought he could control alcohol, it always led him right back to hard drugs and heroin.

In describing his first admission to Quest's Wilson Hall in 2011, he said "I faked it through, saying all the things they wanted me to say, and got Bob as a sponsor", but after getting out some 100 days later, his mom let him return to Columbus and live with her and was soon back with the same friends and people. Again, he thought he could drink, but this soon got out of control and within 10 months he was using heroin again. He made a point of saying how wrong he was about the belief that he could drink. He said he drank "all my mom's liquor", and lost a job for sleeping at work with a hangover, and went to jail for DUI. All of these were consequences of drinking.

When his girlfriend died of a heroin overdose at 21 years old, he knew he had to get back to Stark County to re-connect with his sober network. This did not work, however, as he drove back and forth to Columbus constantly to "buy dope"!

Ryan then told the story of what happened back in July the previous year when he got sober. He had been living with a couple ladies in a part of town that made everyone at the meeting laugh (I took it to mean a part of town that had a reputation for lots of drugs). He told about how his last day of using had come within 12 days after having been arrested in Columbus for violating his probation on a trip home to buy drugs. He went to jail for the weekend, appeared in front of the Drug Court Judge (the one responsible for the probation he "ran from" as he told it. The judge finally decided to kick him out of the drug court program and declare his probation over, because he was violating the spirit of the program by failing to report and follow the rules. (I remembered this decision by the judge at the time to be totally unbelievable—Let him off the hook, declare his probation over and satisfied, when he had done nothing to fulfill the program's requirements. I saw disaster coming and that's what happened, with 12 days!)

Ryan said at this point, July 17, 2012, he only had about 20 bucks to his name (dad had decided not to give him more- how I came to this decision is hard even for me to believe!). He went wandering around Canton, trying to find a store to buy a bottle of booze, as he was starting heroin withdrawal again and didn't have money to buy more. He did, however ingest 7200 mg of an anti-seizure medication called Neurotin that he happened to have, hoping it would do something to make him feel better. He looked up and found himself on the doorsteps of Quest in downtown Canton (he now believes he was led there by God-perhaps the spiritual awakening they talk about in the 12 steps?)

Anyway, while in the process of taking an assessment for the program he had a seizure and fell to his knees. He still has the scars on his knees from falling. He was taken to the hospital twice that day- once by Quest for the seizure, then again by the ladies he was renting the apartment from whe n he returned there and started becoming "abusive" they said, and had another seizure at their house. When he returned to their house later that night, they had kicked him out and had placed all his worldly possessions in his car. Having nowhere else to go, Ryan started driving down to Columbus in an inebriated condition hoping to talk me or his mother to take him in.

He got arrested for his 3rd DUI shortly thereafter having bumped into another car on the freeway and then trying to drive away to avoid getting caught. He was taken to court in Mansfield, Ohio and was given 60 days in jail. The following steps, he believed were all evidence of God's hand at work in his circumstances:

1. He only served 33 days of the 60 day sentence;
2. The Judge allowed him to go back to Stark County to the Quest Wilson Hall program he had done so well in in 2011 (the Probation Officer had told him this Judge never let someone go out of County for treatment. Ryan felt he really needed his support network back in Massillon/Canton);
3. His probation officer told him after the 100 or so days in Wilson Hall he would need to return for his other 27 days—but instead the Judge did something he also never does and counted Ryan's treatment time towards his sentence.

Ryan then talked about what he has been doing since this experience:

1. Attending 5 or 6 AA meetings per week
2. Taking Bob's advice to "pray, read the *Big Book,* go to meetings, help others and "pick up the phone" whenever you are tempted or depressed.

His perspective on the experiences of other sober acquaintances who say they are never tempted again is different. He said the thoughts "still come" and he always picks up the phone He says his rule of thumb has been that if he makes the call, and still feels like getting high afterwards, he has resolved to go to a bar. When he calls Bob, Bob will tell him to wait until Bob gets there and talks to him and if, after that he still feels like drinking, Bob will "go to the bar" with him. Fortunately, these conversations have, in every case, taken away the urge to use substances and normally resulted in attendance at an AA meeting.

Ryan attended Founder's Day (the anniversary of the founding of AA) in Akron, Ohio and bought a key chain of a miniature phone to remind him to make the call. He describes AA as a "simple program for complicated people".

He related how he is proud to say he is now working a full-time job and paying his own rent and bills for the first time in his life. He said that his dad "spent about a quarter of a million dollars supporting him and enabling him over the last 10 years" (I'm not sure exactly where he got that number. It might not be that far off!) He is also proud that he hasn't asked me for money in a year! He said it was the first time he had ever heard of a person getting hired for a job with a reference from a treatment center!

Another interesting aspect of Ryan's "lessons learned" involves having real, true friends for the first time. He said for 9 years he had nothing but drug using buddies. He said these people are not true friends, and that now his program friends are "true friends" The person he believed to be his "best friend" was the guy who showed him how to roll his first joint, how to take cocaine and taught him to shoot heroin. He also told how recently this same "friend had called him up and asked to move in with Ryan. As much as he would like to help this guy, he had to tell him "no", because he knew his sobriety would be in danger if he lived with this "friend".

This was quite an emotional experience for me and a happy one. Many friends in the program then got up and thanked Ryan for his Lead and told what things resonated with them.

One complimented Ryan on his public speaking skills as well as his inspiring message, and told him he could be a "professional speaker". Another said he had just experienced a "front row seat to a miracle".

One of the most meaningful comments, to me, was from a young alcoholic who also had just reached 1 year in recovery. He said, as an alcoholic he was doing "something legal" and therefore looked down his nose at drug users. He said he had come to realize that all these addictions are the same, describing it as a "disease of more". By this he meant that whatever made him feel good at the moment, he wanted more of it. Whether it was alcohol, sex, gambling, whatever gave him a rush of good feelings, he concluded if one felt good, "I wanted 20"! There is no difference whatever if it's drugs, alcohol, or many other things people get addicted to. This latter point, to me was very poignant. I wonder how many people in our society and our country are addicted to material things, their jobs and any number of other things we strive for to make us feel better while leaving out our spiritual development. *The Big Book of Alcoholics Anonymous* describes addiction as a spiritual disease.

CONCLUSION

WHAT HAVE I LEARNED?

I have learned a lot from my journey with my son in his addiction. If anything I have learned can help other parents going through what I did, then I can do some good in the world. Maybe I'll save a kid's life, maybe a parent's sanity! I think it's that serious. Here are just some of the learnings:

1. I, as a parent, have no control over addiction.
2. I cannot solve someone else's addiction. It will only happen, if at all, when the addict realizes, himself, that he needs to get sober.
3. I do not know what it might take for an addict to get the point where he wants to get sober.
4. In my experience, if I could predict, it may and probably will require some pretty terrible consequences to happen in the addict's life to get them to the point of desperately wanting sobriety. (Maybe what I think is terrible is just what is needed)
5. I can stand in the way of terrible things from happening, and by so doing, may just risk my child's life.
6. It may take just as long for me to "get it" as the addict, and I may have to experience as many terrible things in my life to "get it"!

7. Trying to shield my kid from pain and consequences can stand in the way of his wanting to get sober and will prolong the problem.

We say all the time in our Nar-Anon meetings that we are not to give advice to other parents, because everyone is on his or her own journey and will get to where they need to be in their own time and when they are ready. But, a few words of wisdom from one who has tried, failed and taken many years to "get it":

> Join a Nar-Anon or Al-Anon group and keep going. It will be hard at first and take a long time, but your life will improve.

> Treat yourself as worthy of having a good life.

> Even if the worst happens, you will get through it with God's help.

> Most importantly, positive things only began to happen for my son when I "got out of they way" and turned him over to God!

www.ingramcontent.com/pod-product-compliance
Lightning Source LLC
LaVergne TN
LVHW041612070526
838199LV00052B/3106